For all those who help others make their dreams come true.

Healing Wisdom
for a
Wounded World

My Life-Changing Journey Through a Shamanic School

Book 4

WEAM NAMOU

HERMiZ
PUBLiSHING

Library of Congress Cataloging-in-Publication Data
2016915537

Namou, Weam
ISBN 978-1-945371-94-3

Healing Wisdom for a Wounded World
My Life-Changing Journey Through a Shamanic School
Book 4
(memoir)

First Edition

Published in the United States of America by:
Hermiz Publishing, Inc.
Sterling Heights, MI

10 9 8 7 6 5 4 3 2 1

Contents

Chapter 1
QUIT TRYING TO QUIT

On the last day of January, Lynn gathered her apprentices for a conference call to celebrate all of our accomplishments from the previous year and welcome in the New Year. With a hoarse, coughing voice, she acknowledged how hard it is for people to delve into the core of their being. Each apprentice had created an abundant spirit by stepping on a path that's very difficult but very fun. She did so with the support of other sisters who worked with her, honored her, and shared her journey as she left the valley and decided to climb back up the mountain.

"This creates a really special bond that few people ever have," she said. "There are many schools in the world where you can learn about all kinds of wonderful things, but I don't know where you find anything quite as deeply personal as this, where you go in and find your failings and frailties."

She said that we have now accomplished great things and are part of a grand circle of wisdom, beauty, and comfort that has been spinning throughout time for many histories. Then she instructed us to do an act of power ceremony. The greatest act of power, in her opinion, was to dedicate ourselves to the process of enlightenment, to open our hearts and learn to be free.

"The only things that keep you from being free are the attachments, the way you've been conditioned as a child by your

1

family and society," she said. "Keep the things you like but give away the negative feelings, like unworthiness, because they no longer belong to you."

We were to create a circle using four stones, sit in the center, and then move around the wheel. Starting with the south, we had to ask ourselves as we prayed to the Great Spirit, "What have I accomplished physically? What have I overcome? What was I lax on? What should I have done that I didn't do?"

Then turning to the west, we had to think of our sacred dream and ask ourselves, "What did I dream that this life was going to be and how have I fulfilled that dream, or not?"

"If you feel you're far away from your dream, if you haven't manifested your dreams, you need to look at that and own it so that you can shift it. Do this while you're in the school and you have the strength to do it," she said. "Imagine you are sitting in a place where you are living your dream."

She gave the example of being an insurance salesperson when what you love to do is art. The two jobs have different frequencies, so to get closer to your dream, you have to move toward the frequency of being an artist. Initially, you'll worry that you won't make money as an artist, and probably in the beginning, you won't. However, you can work on your dream and sell insurance at the same time. A year later, you would have shifted frequencies a great deal and would be closer to your dream. It's the same with money. People who feel that money is short need to move from that frequency over to great abundance.

After visiting the west, we were to move to the north on the wheel, to Spirit, and ask, "What has been my inspiration in the last year? How has the school empowered me? Have I lost or gained inspiration? What is the wisdom behind what I've gained and how has wisdom worked for me, or has it not worked for me in the way I wanted or needed it to?"

"I can't imagine that it's not working on you, but maybe it isn't," Lynn said. "It would be good to take a look at how you perceive the reality of your wisdom. Wisdom comes in in so many different ways, and it's difficult to see at times."

After visiting the west, we were to move to the east, where the mind lives, and ask ourselves, "Is my decision rational? Am I making a decision that will be helpful for me?" The critic also lives in the east, and it might tell us that we're just wasting our time, to go get a job. The critic doesn't have a soul, is very cold, and just wants us to make money. The Old Wise One is another part of the east, and it might say, "You are fantastic, and you're doing the things that feed your soul. There are not many things in this world that feeds your soul."

"Beauty is the food of the soul, and if you are creating beauty you are creating sustenance for the spirit that will keep you whole and strong," Lynn said.

Finally there is the sacred clown in the east, the trickster that will try to dissuade you from any decision that you make. It's his way of testing you to see if your decision is strong.

Someone on the call, a man from a different school year, brought up the story of his pygmy goat, a pet he had as a child which ended up dying. He loved it very much and recently the goat came to his mind through a fortune teller. He wanted to know how he could transform the grief and sadness into gratitude, gratitude for, at least, having had his little pygmy goat.

"You learn tremendously through grief," Lynn said. "It deepens and changes you forever, and it gives you an understanding that death is really an ally. The goal is not to round your shoulder and close your heart chakra but to realize that life and death is a cycle and it's a gift. When someone is dying, you have a great respect for what they're going through and you don't want to minimize it, but through great compassion, you can also help them move into a place that is the beginning of a new process of life. In the death is the seed of the next success."

She talked a little about the Alaskan seven-day holistic cruise in June, where she was one of nearly two dozen spiritual teachers and healers to lecture, lead workshops, and host private sessions. In August she was leading a journey to ancient Peru. Because of these trips, there would not be a Joshua Tree event this year. Lynn had mentioned last year at Storm Eagle that she wanted to venture into other parts of the world for the gatherings, that maybe from now on we would have Storm Eagle abroad. This idea terrified me because it would require a lot more travel time. I was finally graduating and didn't want any complications that would cause me to go through the same struggles I had gone through before.

At the end of the call, Lynn said she wanted to offer for the New Year a prayer for abundance of spirits in the physical world. I was nearly drifting off at this point when suddenly the word "money" woke me up. She said, "Money is the trade beads of the twentieth century. Great Spirit, how may I better string the beads of abundance in my life? Often I have thought that money was an evil thing and I have been afraid to accumulate any kind of wealth, but now I understand that you have given me a great teaching, that I am worthy of comfort and warmth in the evening when it is cold, that I do not have to go without to be a sacred being.

"I have worked hard in my life," she continued to pray. "I have been afraid to be paid for my efforts because I thought it was wrong but I was the one who was wrong, Great Spirit. I took your gifts and threw them back in your face, but the gift of abundance is the same as the gift of the sacred pipe or the energy that abounds in a newborn child. All the energy of the earth is from you, Great Spirit, so for me to turn my back on your gifts is an insult. I thank you for helping me understand that we are, indeed, all one on this great earth, and as I become abundant I help others become abundant. If you give to me, it does not make someone else less fortunate. Quite the contrary, it gives those lacking the courage to follow their dreams the ability to manifest in their lives all that they need."

Her words poured over me like an invigorating sauce. They stirred my emotions, my desire to move forward, until I felt warm, then hot, then anxious. For years, I've tried to take off, to fly, but I've always failed. My spirit grew frustrated, got drained by the routine of writing, of editing, revising, submitting, repeat, yet I was unable to feel success, a success which, to me, meant a total contentment for what I have and who I am.

Was my ambition beyond my reach? Should I reevaluate my goals? Do I have a fear of the heights of success? My most laborious efforts have not steered me into success. Should I quit? Can I even quit? These questions sometimes snuck into my mind, and then, just as she did in today's closing prayer, Lynn would tell me that I could not avoid where I was heading and that I ought to quit trying to quit.

woolen *adj* made of wool. * *n* cloth made of wool.

woolgathering *n* idle dreaming.

word *n* an articulate sound expressing an idea; information; a saying; motto; promise; *pl* a quarrel; *pl* lyrics. * *vt* to put into words; to flatter.

wording *n* the mode of expressing in words.

wordy *adj* using many words; verbose.

work *n* effort; employment; a task; achievement; a book or other composition; a factory. * *vi* to labor, toil; to be employed; to ferment. * *vt* to bring

worship *n* religious servic reverence; title of honor. to perform religious ser

worshipful *adj* honorable

worst *adj* bad or evil in * *vt* to defeat.

worsted *n* woolen yarn

worth *adj* equal in valu * *n* value; price.

worthy *adj* deserving notable person.

would-be *adj* wishin

wound *n* a cut or s *vi* to inflict a wou

wove *pl* of **weave**.

wrack *n* seaweed g

Chapter 2
THE WORD *WORD*

It was a full moon in February. All of Lynn's apprentices around the world were asked to join the dreamtime for a thirty-minute meditation which began at 9 pm each person's time. We had to find a quiet place in which to sit or lie down, close our eyes, take a few deep breaths, relax, and allow our energy to connect with the energy of mother earth. In the mythology of some Australian Aborigines, dreamtime refers to the "time before time" or "the time of creation of all things." Dreamtime stories, which explain life and its idiosyncrasies, differ from region to region and from people to people. Some talk about legends and the ancestors. Others talk about the stars and supernatural realms. It is a state of being where you encompass the past, present, and future at the same time.

Since the full moon is a good time to clear out what no longer serves us, to let go, Lynn wanted us to meditate on what we wanted or needed to release in the beginning of this year's study. I decided to let go of my career, the title of a writer. Lynn had often said, "You are not what you do," and yet somewhere along the path, the title of a writer had become my identity. What originated as a love, passion, and calling became a burden and an attachment. I spent nearly twenty-five years of stacking bricks upon bricks to create a beautiful and meaningful building, yet, for whatever reason, I was unable to find a way to build the ceiling. The building had a strong foundation and stood tall, like the Ishtar Gate, one of many walls that surrounded and protected Babylonia from outside forces. This gate was constructed in about 575 BC by order of King Nebuchadnezzar II and dedicated to the Babylonian Ishtar, goddess of fertility, love, war, and sex. The gate was considered one of the original Seven Wonders of the World, but it was later replaced on that list by the Lighthouse of Alexandria from the third century BC.

A tall building without a roof has a lot of empty space. During rain storms it can hold enough water to create a beach. In winter season, it can capture mounds of snow. Depending on the weather, anything can fall in it and so the builder, while stacking the bricks, has to also clean it up regularly. The rigorous task becomes more difficult the higher the building reaches and the hollower its interior becomes. More tools – shovels, brooms, buckets, strength – are needed. Hitting against it with something like a hammer will not make a ceiling appear. Neither will pleading or negotiating with it. Telling it, "Hasta la vista, baby!" would do the trick. It'd get you to throw down the towel, turn around, and follow a different path, or no path at all. Doing nothing is a lot of fun, honest to goodness! To simply lie in the fields all day, gaze at the clouds, and fall asleep to the sound of birds chirping, trees and flowers breathing, and children playing in the background. By doing nothing physically, you could still add more light and love to the world.

There was enormous relief in the prospect of doing nothing as I dove into the fourth-year school material, called *Lodge of the Spirit*, biting each word on the page like a chipmunk. The words tasted incredibly yummy, and it actually had nutrients that created a euphoric high. This intense state of happiness and contentment began to shrivel up as the pages revealed words which seemed to have less nutritional value because they pointed at our inner dark side. Lynn said not to let our energy fall as we approach the finish line.

Fourth year was about bringing all of our tools and talents together, specifying our vision, and setting our course into the world. It was about the completion/creation cycle. The movement was from spirit in the north to manifestation in the south. As I read this, Storm Eagle came to mind. At last year's event, there were separate areas set up for apprentices to learn the differences between being a dreamer, seer, stalker, or conjuror. The mentors and their assistants shared their experiences with us and they explained how each direction differed from the other. They said that, regardless of how we moved energy, we all had the ability to hone and use the skills associated with the south, west, north, and east.

One of the mentors used the story of fishing to explain each direction. First, you dream up the idea of wanting to eat fish for dinner. Second, you set your intent with spirit to go catch some fish. Third, you stalk your idea – plan, gather your tools, and go out to the lake, river, or pond. Fourth, you catch the fish, bring it home, and cook it. Dinner is served. The dream is manifested and the circle is complete.

My dream was still in the womb. The manuscript had gone through the dream, the spirit, and the stalking stages, but it had not manifested into book form. And here was Lynn telling me that I must be impeccable as an apprentice. To move forward, to take my power, finishing projects was essential to my journey as an apprentice. Worst of all, she wanted me to work with words! I didn't even want to say the word *word*. Words were beginning to feel like ants, millions of them, crawling into my body. Their occupancy reminded me of what happened last year, when bird mites, after the newborn birds outside our home abandoned their nests, searched for a new host to feed on.

Someone had placed my sandals on the porch beneath the nest, which had shed twigs, grass, and mud onto them. I brought the sandals inside to the laundry room's sink, and as faucet water flowed over them, tiny black dots suddenly appeared on my hands and quickly sprouted like a flower onto my arms. I quickly washed them off with soap and got rid of the bird nest. But then I suffered from extreme itching, crawling sensations, and abrupt isolated prickles that went on for several days as I tried to remove the thousands of bird mites with tea tree, coconut oil, olive oil, and Epsom salt.

Bird mites die within three weeks without a blood meal from a bird host and cannot survive on humans for extended periods of time. Not wanting to infest our home, children, and car, I washed the laundry, secluded myself, and stood in front of the bathroom mirror for hours, carefully rubbing my body with various oils. The teachings became quite clear. I hadn't looked at myself in the mirror for a long, long time, my eyes always darting away like a bunny playing in the fields. Even when penciling my eyelids with liquid liner, my focus was on the shape I drew. My eagerness to make the beds, cook dinner, write the next chapter, pay the bills, clean up after the kids, get to a yoga class or this and that meeting kept me from appreciating my body and treating it with love and admiration. We tell our children that they are beautiful, magnificent, magical, and miraculous beings and we forget to take the time to tell ourselves that.

Staring into the mirror, my eyes and I became so intimate, I lost track of time and diminished into an old soul who rarely allowed her true self to be seen in the world. We wear so many masks throughout the day that we forget what we look like without them, without this façade. For some it's too horrifying to remove these masks, to see what's underneath, and yet, if we keep wearing them, we will ultimately become overwhelmed, sad, and disconnected from our spirit. I thanked the mites for this lesson, and they left.

Lynn asked that we write our favorite words across a page, some big, some small, sideways, or backwards, using different colors; say the word out loud, then say the words in another language, then say them in an invented language; to do this over and over again, every day and every night. But Lynn, I wanted to say, I'm sick of words! I've had enough of them to last me ten lifetimes! Millions of words had crossed my fingertips as I repeatedly wrote, revised, and edited.

She said that we had come to this teaching over a path created by words, literally a bridge of words that allowed and invited us to enter into her world and the world of the Sisterhood. She also said that shamans had, throughout time, healed with words, with stories, with phrases and sounds derived from unknown languages from secret worlds. So she asked us to write and analyze several stories and I thought, dear God, no! No more stories! Enough already!

Then I came across a website, Tengerism.org, which explains the different kinds of shamans and other spiritual callings. The bonesetter's main work is setting bones and fixing dislocations. It is said that a bonesetter can see a broken bone as accurately as an x-ray machine. They use mentally dissociative states and spirit helpers in their healing work but are unable to master spirits. This calling is inherited from the paternal line. In most tribes, only men can be bonesetters because bones are considered the masculine part of the body.

My father was the head of the accounting department at Baghdad's railroad station. For additional income, he translated and interpreted Arabic to English and English to Arabic. At night, he was a bonesetter. People with broken bones or sprained muscles or ligaments came to him rather than going to a doctor or the hospital. He treated them for free. As soon as the patient arrived, my mother filled the laundry tub with warm water and brought it to the living room along with towels and a big, hard, green bar of soap made of olive oil and other ingredients which everyone in Iraq used to wash their hands, body, and hair. The soap smelled delicious and was good for the hair and skin. It even helped remove acne. When working on someone, he immediately knew what type of fracture it was and whether the person had to go to the hospital.

There is the midwife, whose job is part physical and part spiritual. A midwife invokes the spirits in her work. Hassina, my paternal aunt, was a midwife. A widow with one son, she was one of the few Christians living in the Muslim city of Falluja. She'd studied nursing and used her skills to heal people and save a number of lives, especially newborn girls. Long ago, when Fallujah was just a small town, it was customary amongst Arab tribes for the father, if he so desired, to bury a newborn girl. Some men wanted to do just that, but my aunt was such an educated, smart, and compassionate woman that she was able to convince them not to. With an effective tongue, she used anecdotes from their Quran because Islam forbids these acts. In the Quran, it is said that on Judgement Day, buried girls will rise out of their graves and ask for what crime they were killed.

There are the healers, which, unlike the bonesetters and midwives, do not inherit their calling from family lines but from the will of the spirits. Called *otoshi* in Mongolian, they are almost always females, although males have also been called. They specialize in fertility and child health issues but also tend to other physical ailments. They have always been strong feminists.

This would be my great great grandmother, Maria, a legend in her time. She was a powerful healer and businesswoman. Like all early societies, ancient Mesopotamians attributed sickness to spiritual causes. There were three types of medical practitioners. There was the sorcerer, or witch doctor. He diagnosed the ailment and determined which god or demon was causing the illness and whether the disease was the result of some error or sin on the part of the patient. Then there was the exorcist. He prescribed charms and spells that were designed to drive out the spirit causing the disease, and if need be, referred the patient to a physician. The physician used herbal remedies, applied bandages, and performed minor surgeries. Maria was not only a healer but a feminist. She rode horses in the desert when women were not supposed to do so.

The shaman's assistant is a spiritual person without a specific calling. That describes one of my six sisters. Then there is the shaman smith, and he makes and empowers a shaman's equipment. Clairvoyants are seers who practice divination, some by going into a trance and others by having visions. They are in tune with the spirits and can tell people about the future. There's also the bard, whose job is to keep the cultural traditions, history, and legends alive through storytelling and song.

I finally began to understand, to see how I fit into this circle of shamans. I had walked into Lynn's den without knowing who she was or what shamanism meant. I thought she was simply an author helping other authors and creative beings excel. I thought shamanism was just a word to describe Native Americans of a certain tribe. Had I known the real definition, I would have run the opposite direction. My calling had pursued me in the subtlest way, through writing, to get me to remember who I really am without words and to make it clear why words are needed to serve the grander cause of allowing my people to have a voice and be represented truthfully. Further, through words, I could honor Enheduanna, the princess, high priestess, and earliest known writer in history who was dubbed as the "Shakespeare of Sumerian literature." Using first person in her sophisticated and exceptionally personal writings, she displayed her sentiments, spiritual views, and political rebellion. As a result, she was driven from the temple and exiled to the prairies. Although she was a genius who survived and returned to her position at the Ur sacred temple, her importance in the world, in history books and legendary tales, has been conveniently left out.

Chapter 3
MY LAST MENTOR

This was Nancy's first year mentoring. She graduated with Leslie years ago and had not been to any of the gatherings for nearly ten years. She learned about the Sisterhood of the Shields in 1984, when a friend suggested she read *Medicine Woman*. She read it and thought, "This is a crazy story."

"But it grabbed me," she told me over the phone during our first conversation. "I also thought, why is Lynn asking so many questions? I didn't ask questions because I was hiding. One day I found out that Lynn would be at a Spirit Expo in Seattle, so I went. I waited until she was done speaking and when I approached her to give her a gift, she was delighted and gave me a little hug. I was surprised by her kind reaction. It was after that that I went to the Joshua Tree event."

She talked about her experience as a fourth-year apprentice, how this was the year she had pulled it all together.

"This is a circular, nonlinear teaching," she said.

Linear is learning mostly through constricted educational systems whereas non-linear learning occurs more naturally and is often based on creativity. Lynn describes the teachings of the Sisterhood as holographic and three-dimensional, where the past, present, and future all exist simultaneously as our reality. This theory goes back to the ancient indigenous people who believed that we exist in a dream or illusion and that reality, as we consciously experience it, is not real.

"Here, you visit the issues over and over again," Nancy said. She had an energetic and lively voice. Something about her was very open, not at all reserved, and it made me feel comfortable, like I could talk to her as a friend and not a mentor. "We're not just doing assignments and turning them in. We're working on ourselves. I'm an artsy crafty person, so second year I started to feel resistance to the teachings. When I got to Storm Eagle, my drum was still wet and soggy and it didn't drum right. I had to use a hairdryer in my hotel room to dry it."

I then told her my story, how I had discovered Lynn's work through the book *Writing Spirit* and later signed up for the school in order to move my writing career forward.

"Despite the incredible accomplishments and changes that occurred the last three years, I suddenly felt frustrated when reading the fourth-year material," I said. "I'm almost ready to give up chasing this dream of mine, of finding the right people to work with and making a good living from my writing career. I've written the book and submitted query letters and book proposals to agents and publishers. There's nothing left for me to do. I just don't know where this is going anymore."

"That will be discovered if you let it go for a little while. You need to step away from it. Since I stopped working for a living, for money, things have fallen into place. You know, I paint and sometimes when I get stuck trying to complete a painting, I turn it upside down and go from there. You have to turn your view of this upside down."

"Yes, I realize my challenge this year is to truly let it go."

"You sound like an amazingly accomplished person, and your path is very much established. This year is designed to help you come out into the world. Sometimes we have to shed things, and it might come back in a different form. I love your story. It's very inspiring. When I saw your picture on Facebook, I wondered where you were from. I thought, maybe you're Native American."

Sitting on my bed, I took a good, hard look at myself in the mirror.

"When we let things go, they don't disappear," she said. "They're just there to twirl around and appear later at the right time."

"I need to trust this to the Great Spirit."

"It's too wild to contain. Just let it go and be in the background. It'll emerge when you're ready and it's ready. There's a difference between letting it go and throwing it away. I'm sixty-three years old, and I've been married for almost thirty years. I noticed that if I go back to my earliest childhood, I remember back in New York I was looking at a book about national parks in Washington. Forty years later I'm living in Washington, a few miles from the park, after having lived in Alaska for twenty years. The older we get, the more we see."

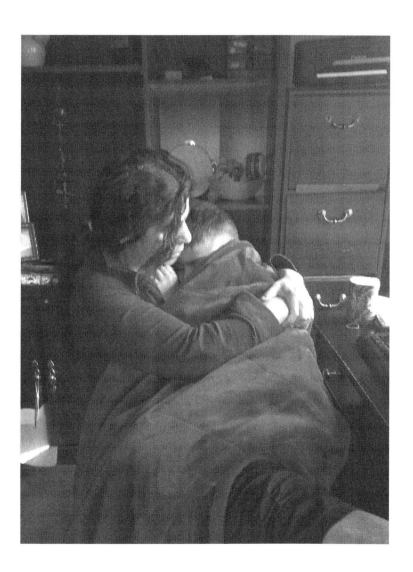

Chapter 4:
NOT MARRYING THE OUTCOME

Within a week, the apprentices had another conference call with Lynn. She talked about how scientists today are just picking up what ancient teachings knew thousands of years ago about black holes and white holes. Of course, she was right. Many ancient societies were in fact more advanced than us. Otherwise, how would they have built pyramids and other monuments through techniques too complex for us to figure out despite decades of scientific research and the help of technology?

My birth country, which today resembles a hell on earth, has several wonders of the world. Through a laborious and resolute construction endeavor, King Nebuchadnezzar helped transform Babylonia into the height of a powerful ancient civilization. Not only were temples restored to their prior glory, but he began two of the most prominent projects of ancient Mesopotamia: Ishtar Gate and the Hanging Gardens of Babylon.

Ishtar Gate, one of many thresholds that surrounded and protected Babylonia from outside forces, was so magnificently built that it made the initial list of the Seven Wonders of the Ancient World, but it was later replaced by the Lighthouse of Alexandria. Some authors wrote that the Ishtar Gate should still be considered one of the wonders. Dedicated to Ishtar, the

Babylonian goddess of fertility, love, war, and sex, this gate pays homage to other deities through various animal representations such as young bulls, lions, and dragons.

The Hanging Gardens is one of the Seven Wonders of the World. The Gardens feature an ascending series of tiered gardens containing all kinds of trees, shrubs, and vines. The Garden, which was destroyed in an earthquake in second century BC, is said to have looked like a large green mountain constructed of mud bricks. It is believed to have been a remarkable achievement of engineering. Most scholars believe that Nebuchadnezzar II had this garden built for his wife from Medina, Queen Amytis, because she missed the green hills and valleys of her homeland.

According to the historian A. Aaboe, Babylonian astronomy was the first and highly successful attempt at giving a refined mathematical description of astronomical phenomena. Babylonians exhibited amazing talent, magic, mysticism, astrology, and divination. The region was a spring of civilization, the womb of cultural evolution. Historians reflected upon its beginnings with admiration and respect. Yet look at them now! Centuries of pillaging and destruction have brought this land to its knees, and today it has little resemblance to its rich past.

My thoughts strenuously crawled away from that world of pain and sorrow. I wished I could remove Iraq's skeletons from my body and throw them away like I would old, dingy dresses.

When my mind returned to the call, Lynn was responding to a woman's question. "As you understand what happened to you in childhood and you forgive those who hurt you, you become warmer and you begin to melt," she said. "Your ego mind, your conditioned mind, wants to prevent you from going after your career. It wants to hold you back from attaining happiness. Instead of being upset about it, move into love and gratitude.

Thank God, the Great Spirit, for the opportunity to learn something important. The only thing to go after is your very best, so why not adopt gratitude and generosity as your role model?"

She also said, "You become free by letting things go that have hurt you all of your life."

The questions and answers continued, and as I became somewhat inattentive, I wrapped the red blanket closer around me as I lay on the couch. Then Lynn said, "With all the wars in this world, we're lucky to be living in this country. I believe the world is going to be saved by the women of the West."

I'd never heard her say that before, but she was right. Many societies have thrived as a result of powerful women, even Mesopotamia. Kubaba, a Sumerian Queen in ancient Iraq, is the world's first recorded woman ruler in history. She was said to have reigned peacefully for one hundred years. Matriarchal communities existed in the past, and there are a number of them surviving today. One society in the high mountains of China is known as the Kingdom of Women. Their reputation for "free love," along with the breathtaking landscape of their homelands, draws increasing numbers of tourists.

Jennifer Morse writes in her book *Apprentice to Power*, the following conversation she had with Lynn, where Lynn says, "The nature of the earth is feminine, so we women naturally understand the nature of things. Deep down, each woman knows that she knows, but we are taught that we don't know. For men, the energy of this planet is not familiar. So they don't know, but they are taught that they know."

"So it's all set up backwards," Jennifer said.

Lynn smiled. "Yes, it is. We have to teach them."

Perhaps this explains the thousands of years of unnecessary wars and violence. The biggest difference between matriarchal and patriarchal communities is that where women rule, there was and is no need for violence. Unnecessary violence is prevalent amongst chimpanzees, who differ from human DNA by just over one percent, and are male dominated. Chimpanzees engage in violence and wars. Yet their close cousins, the bonobos, live a peaceful life because of their matriarchal society. The bonobos have the reputation as the "make love, not war" member of the ape lineage. Maybe that's the core problem in the Middle East. It is overly male dominated, which has created an incredible imbalance in that region.

I felt grateful for the dozens of powerful Western women who had supported my work throughout the years, and I wouldn't be a bit surprised if Western women, like Lynn said, end up saving the world. They have made leaps in attaining their power through economic, sexual, and reproductive freedom. They have a voice and are in a position to be influential in their communities. They have the opportunity to reach out to their women counterparts in the East and help on a global scale. They operate from a place of unity and not excessive individuality. With them in power, there's the potential to end this nasty habit of war.

I wondered if the purpose of these ancient teachings was to Westernize me so that I could one day help heal the part of the world I was trying to run away from. Why else would I have been born there, then come here, and yet continue to be stranded in that nether world between here and there? Each time I try to put off sparks produced by good or bad events that take place in Iraq, these sparks turn into flames in my heart.

Lynn told us a story about how, one day, she'd heard a voice say to her, "Get out of the way of God." She realized it was the Great Spirit telling her to get out of her own away. Lynn said,

"Once you decide what you want in this life, let go of your attachment to it. If you're taking things too seriously, it wouldn't hurt you to talk to Ruby Plenty Chief or Twin Dreamers to see the humor and look at thngs differently. Call upon any women from the Sisterhood."

"Lynn, how can I work on a project and yet be detached from it?" I asked.

"Because you're not married to the outcome," she said. "Oh, it's got to be this way or that way and nothing else. You go out there and do what you do best and don't worry about it. Don't become married to the outcome. Trust that everything will happen as it should. Tell the Great Spirit, I need your grace to finish and to make this whole project beautiful and wonderful. I know you know better how to do it than I do, and so I give it over to you."

The next woman asked, "How do I let go of fear, the fear of trusting my own judgment?"

I did not listen to the answer, having been fully satisfied with the answer Lynn had given to my question. I decided to go out there and do what I do best, write, and not to worry about the outcome.

Chapter 5
ANCIENT WISDOM COUNCIL

I learned at Storm Eagle that there were no councils of the Whistling Elk in Michigan, so I decided to start one myself. I called it the Ancient Wisdom Council. Having savored the experience of a shamanic community in-person, I wanted to replicate that at home, even if on a much smaller scale. Plus, time spent on the council could be used for experiential hours.

The first few meetings, we gathered at the local library. It was mostly myself, my nieces, my sister, and another woman. My wish was to meet at my home with the presence of my mother and my children so that they would naturally benefit from and learn these teachings. Concerned who would show up at my door, I kept the invitations to family in the beginning. One of my nieces warned me about this idea, said that the sisters that had never shown interest in spiritual work had the tendency to turn a simple gathering into a dramatic affair.

I knew this was true, but I did not feel right about excluding anyone and I had a deep longing to strengthen my relationship with my sisters, make it whole again. Although we were on good terms, we'd started to behave more like acquaintances than sisters. I wanted us to re-bond and enjoy each other's company while mom was still alive. She was the glue that held the family together, and now she was once again in the hospital. She'd used her arm strength to wriggle around the bed railing, fell out of the bed, and fractured her hip.

On Valentine's Day, she had called my name in the middle of the night and when I went to open the door, I couldn't. Her body was on the ground, her head right behind the door, jamming it shut. My husband immediately came to help. Since he's skinnier than me, he squeezed sideways through the slightly open door. Once we were both inside, we tried to figure out how to lift her. She was face down, and when my husband tried to touch her shoulders, she cried in pain. He asked me, "What do you want to do?"

"Let's think this through so she does not get hurt."

"Okay, so do you want me to pick her up?"

"Didn't I just say let's think this through?"

"All we have to do is pick her up."

"Don't rush this. How are you going to pick her up with her lying on her stomach like that? We have to at least turn her over on her back."

I placed pillows under her head as we turned her over, then we got her to sit on the wheelchair. She cried that she had leg pain, and I prayed she had not broken anything. We went into the kitchen. My husband made himself a drink, sat in the living room, and turned on the television. I sliced Spanish cheese and served it to her with pita bread. She said she did not want to eat. Her face quivered from fear and excitement. She ended up eating very little and when we took her to her bed, I noticed her left leg was limp. It took a lot of effort to put her in bed. In the morning, when I tried to settle her into the wheelchair, her knees buckled and I had to lay her safely on the ground. I called the ambulance, and a new ordeal resumed due to my mom needing hip surgery and my family members' schedules when it came to hospital visiting hours.

I tried to keep it together and to look at what was import-ant. I worried that once my mother was gone we, the siblings, would not be able to repair our relationship. There would be no reason for us to even try. I wanted to try my best to avoid this, so for the next council meeting, rather than have it at the library, I went ahead and invited my sisters and nieces, about a dozen of them, over my house.

Given my mother's hospitalization, I believed that noth-ing would cause us to quarrel. This was the moment I had been waiting for, the moment where I could collect the spiritual tools I'd accumulated in the past three years and wrap them around us like a big fat Band-Aid. We would sit around the fireplace and have a Kumbaya experience in a Zen atmosphere. This is the type of thing that Native Americans, the Sisterhood of the Shields, did within their communities. They gathered around and honored each other's strengths and listened to or tried to help each other. I wanted this experience to be warm and loving and, like cookies baking in the oven, to spread tasty scents and memories throughout the house to the hearts of our children.

My husband brought home pizza with delightful vegetarian toppings. Everyone arrived on time, carrying a variety of dishes from dolma to saffron rice, kabobs, potato curry, mini cakes, strawberries, and blueberries. I started the fireplace and burned incense, the children went into their rooms to play with their cousins, and the adults sat in the living room, a plate of food on their laps or the table in front of them. The smell of burning wood, incense, and the aroma of ethnic spices, including car-damom tea, created a high temperature. The room became hot and delicious.

At six o'clock I summoned everyone to sit in the living

room, where I dimmed the lights so that mostly the fireplace lit the cold, winter night. The loud volume in the room took a while to mellow. Some of the women threw away their paper plates while others got into a comfortable position. The flames and crackling sound from the fireplace became more prominent. Complete silence otherwise. The zeal and love in the room generated in me a bottomless appreciation for this opportunity. We were together again, this time not engaged in drama but rather prayer and meditation.

My niece placed her toddler on her lap, her arms wrapped around him like a blanket. I led some breathing exercises, and then we entered a meditation. Halfway into it, we were beautifully interrupted by the sound of my niece's toddler son, who observed us with awe and deliberately yelled "Oooo!" during our deepest silence. We laughed, embraced his cute behavior, and returned to our breathing.

After the meditation, I provided notebooks for the women who had not brought one and asked them to list ten things that they liked about themselves and ten things that they did not like about themselves. This was an exercise that my former teachers, Chip and Susan, had their students do. Chip was a Native American man from the Cherokee tribe and his companion, Susan, was part-French, part-Native American.

"I don't know what to write," one of my sisters said while the others were reflecting and writing down their thoughts.

"Write anything that you like about yourself," I said.

"Anything like what?"

"Things that you consider are good qualities," my niece said to her.

"Yes, what are your good qualities?" someone else asked.

"Well, I'm not the one to make that judgement," my sister

said. "That would be self-delusion. I can't, for instance, say I'm this or that about myself because that might not be so. People might have other perceptions of me. They might not consider me a good listener and yet I'm considering myself a good listener. Others should be the judge of my good qualities."

"But in this exercise, write what *you* like about yourself," I said. "It has nothing to do with how others view you."

"That makes no sense at all! I could have the impression that I'm a caring, loving person but in actuality I'm not. My spouse might think I'm quite the opposite, that I'm a mean-spirited and selfish person. So who is right or wrong in this case?"

"You're overthinking this," I said. "There are plenty of wonderful things about you, such as, you're an honest, hardworking person, and you are a great mother. You love your job, you love going for walks, you enjoy the simple things in life, and you are a very good cook…"

She smiled at the list. "Yeah, that's true." She wrote a few things down and then again brought up her point that other peoples' perception of you is important and could even be more accurate.

When we moved on to the list of things we disliked about ourselves, she again had an issue. What should she write? What were her negative qualities? With these questions, there were volunteers galore offering to chip in and help her realize her negative attributes. As they handed out their lists, she became defensive and, as the facilitator, I said that we did not need to misuse this time by pointing out other peoples' faults. The slight tension that arose quickly melted away, and I explained that they should keep their list of things they liked about themselves and destroy the list of things they disliked about themselves by either throwing it into a fire or a bowl of water. Watching it burn

31

to ashes or disintegrate in the water, they would give thanks for having experienced whatever they disliked about themselves and then bid it farewell.

The next and last part of the evening was the guided meditation. I chose a meditation from Lynn's book, *The Mask of Power,* which asked the reader to call in the spirit of their mother into their circle then their father. I told them to give a prayer of thanks for however wonderful or difficult their relationship was with their mother or father and listen to the message that parent has for them. "Now listen to the message, the teaching, the wisdom, and give thanks," I said.

I heard sniffling and remembered the reaction these exercises had upon me when I did them months before the first year of the school. The exercises started me on a long and intimate journey with my parents, where we shared sentiments that we had not communicated verbally in the physical world. Through the essence of their spirit, they taught me what I couldn't comprehend through language.

We were doing well, with only a few ladies chattering here and there, and then I asked them to bring their husbands into the circle. All hell broke loose.

"My husband!" one said, astounded.

"Yeah, why are you ruining the mood right now?" another said.

"This is unnecessary, and what's the use of it anyway?"

"Come on, Weam, you were doing so well, and then you have us deal with our husbands!"

"Can you please keep it down because I'm in the middle of a conversation with my husband?" my niece said, frustrated.

Another sister said that she, too, wanted to have a dialogue with her husband and the others were interrupting the process.

Still the interruptions continued, accompanied by giggling. I asked that we please wait until everyone was finished with their experience before we made comments, but the eldest ones decided they weren't going to be told what to do. They kept at it, criticizing these exercises. One called them ridiculous and said she didn't believe in all this crap.

"You don't have to believe in it," I said calmly. "This is just for fun."

She grew angry and threw the notebook on the table, again stating that she did not believe in this. I kept calm, giving her the chance to express herself and realizing that there must be some inner hurt regarding her marriage. Her husband had been disabled for over a decade, and I don't think she ever came to terms with that. Still, the room became hostile as more words of disapproval got tossed around, and soon we tripped into a well of pointy fingers. You did this and that, and how dare you say this and that?

My Zen rope eventually snapped in two, and I lost my temper. I accused this and that person of this and that wrongdoing. This all made the evening perfect, because we were back to our much untamed selves, running wild with our expressions, clawing each other's characters as a form of play. This was the typical rhythm of our gatherings, to where one sister said before leaving my house, "Despite what happened, this was fun."

It was not fun for me. I had spent a lot of time getting the house ready, planning for a beautiful evening, wanting my children to experience the charm of prayer and meditation amongst loved ones. It pained me that it had ended on such a dark note, that I'd said awful things to my sister which I could not take back, that I could not escape from this dreadful role because if I did, their "fun" would discontinue, so it was important that I get pushed and cornered until I behaved as badly as possible so that their "fun" would be complete and I would remain in the same pattern that they could not break free from. I went to bed that night in a complete daze.

I was forewarned, but I didn't listen.

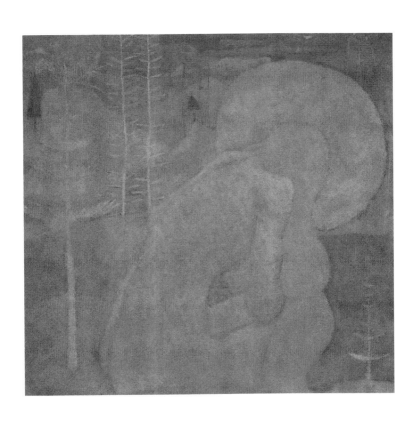

Chapter 6
JUST YOU AND THE CREATOR

In the past, rehab had proved useless for my mother so I told the doctors to send her straight home after she was released from the hospital. They said, "You know she needs two, sometimes even three, people to transport her?"

"Yes," I said.

"Hip procedures take a long time to heal, maybe as long as six months."

"Yes."

"Will you have help at home?"

"Yes."

They arched their brows, puckered their lips, creased the wrinkles between their foreheads, tried to explain the situation more clearly to me, but in the end they shrugged their shoulders. They could not convince me to send her to rehab. The last several times my mother went there, it was more a problem than a solution. The burden of going to visit her fell on me, because well, she lived with me, I did not work out of the home, and historically, I was the designated daughter for that responsibility.

Aside from that, my mother's healing did not begin until she arrived home because she specifically feels as though she must be surrounded by family to heal. So whether she came straight from the hospital or from rehab, Mars, or the moon, she still started from zero, from scratch. I sat my siblings down and explained that I would need their help for one week. By helping me, they would be better off too. Rather than go and visit Mom at rehab, they could spend that time coming to my home. Even if she went to rehab, they would have to help me at my home because, again, my mother's trip to rehab would mean zilch.

The ambulance brought her home one cold February evening, a Friday, and one of the two paramedics handed me a list of medications she would need to take immediately. One was a blood thinner which her pharmacy did not have in stock. They had to order it, and it would not arrive until Monday. I went pharmacy hopping with my son in the backseat until I found someone who could give me enough dosage to last throughout the weekend, and by the time I returned home, my mother was sound asleep. It was 5 pm, and I had a telephone call scheduled with Nancy.

I told her what happened at the council, how the Zen atmosphere had turned turbulent by the end of the night. This had caught me by surprise. I had not thought that we'd once again become the apple of each other's eyes, the way it used to be long ago, but I thought we'd at least like hanging out together. I was also concerned. There was a gut feeling the size of a cantaloupe that we would not be able to move forward.

"I love hearing your story," Nancy said. "It reminds me of someone who kept having conflict with an in-law, and Lynn said to her, 'This is a chance for you to learn about anger and conflict.' Your sister is immersed in competition or something is lacking in her life. Your graciousness in including her could be a wonderful gift. It's a healing. It sounds like your family doesn't always get along. Not everybody is going to understand Lynn's teachings. When I mention anything to my family, outside of my husband and daughters, they don't understand it. They think it's a silly thing."

"I can see how some see my ideas as weird and crazy."

"This is a huge test for you to get what you want," she said. "It's difficult because this is your sister. If it was a stranger, that'd be different. Maybe you can use a talking stick. Then maybe you can contain the criticism or the distraction."

Maybe I could ditch everyone and live happily ever after.

"I can hear the passion, and that's lovely to hear. You're giving your sister a gift, but she has many years of seniority, so there's a control issue. For whatever reason, she might feel that you're trying to one up her, or to make things difficult for her, but that's not the case at all. Perhaps there's something in her where she feels she is never heard. That's why she keeps interrupting. She can't help it. Maybe you can talk to her about this and just know that this is normal life."

A flood of compassion entered my heart. My sister had not been heard and therefore hadn't learned how to deal with energy, emotions, and reactions.

"Things in families are explosive because everyone knows each other so well," she said. "I was so shy because in this country you are taught not to get mad or take it personally, and that prevented me from speaking my mind. Anger wakes up our will. If used correctly, it can get us out of situations that don't serve us."

Her statement woke me up. I had read that anger can reduce violence because it's a social signal that a situation needs to be resolved. It could also provide insight into ourselves and motivate self-change if we notice when we get angry and why. Anger is a way of communicating a sense of injustice. It's a natural response to being systematically oppressed. Aboriginals and people from ethnic cultures, in an attempt to pacify an angry person, will either ignore or agree with everything they say. That, or they'll try to get rid of them without offending them or causing trouble.

"Your guests were a witness to that, and so this experience was a gift for them as well," she said. "Now that you blew up this time then next time you can handle it differently. Give your sister a talking stick, have her talk first, and give her a little more time. You don't want to allow her to be abusive in her behavior, but she might be crying out, 'Hear me! Hear me! I'm a woman in the world who does not know who I am!'"

I talked to the Red Indian about this, and he said, "The clan system holds you back, and most native elders know that. You can't tell younger people that. Some people are seventy years old but actually they're as childish as a twelve-year-old. Yet they think they're the head of the clan. If you tell them they're not the head of the clan, they'll come on you like bricks."

"So how do you handle that?"

"It's not your job to tell them they're not the head of the clan. It's their Creator's job to put it in their mind. If He doesn't put it in their mind then they don't have it anyway. I can tell you all sorts of things, Weam, but unless the Creator shows you, it's not real in your life. You can't help people that don't want the Creator's help. Really, you can't. There are some people who are very, very old who are very, very young spiritually, and the rich ones are the most dangerous because they think they can buy everything, and they can. It's an uncomfortable place, but at the same time, you have to be cordial and understand." He coughed a severe cough. "You have to take it slow. It's fun to talk to someone who understands what you're saying without saying half a sentence. Have you ever run into someone like that?"

"Yes."

"That's what I'm saying. Some people don't understand what you're saying and are older age-wise but much younger spiritually. There are people in your community, in your church, that are running your community, your church, like children. And natives are not any different than other people on the planet earth. But the people who came here and started doing what they were doing, man, they were funny people. They had an agenda, and it was for the riches. It was for the commodities in the ground, and they'd do anything for it.

"People don't want to go to Mars to enjoy the planet, but to take what they can get and get what they want and plunder the entire place and get out of there. They don't even know what they're after, but they want to find out what's up there, and they're spending millions and millions and going around with cruisers and all sorts of crap. To them it's just one big mines project, and they're exactly like the people who came here. They have no intention of living a clean life. They have no intention to live a life of good intentions. Their intention is to get as much as they can get and die doing it."

"Mommy, can I have three birthdays?" my son asked, surprising me. It was after eleven o'clock, and I thought he was already in bed. I told him I'd talk to him about that later, and he walked out of my office.

"Same with the fishermen in Alaska," the Red Indian continued. "They're not out there for a good life. They're not happy until they get all the fish, all the fish, and make lots of money. Whatever they can get. Same with the forests and hunting. And then they put it on TV and think they're real funny and make a big show about it and then they have Tyson chicken advertising while you watch these guys plunder the North continent and they think they're all fine."

I listened attentively as I typed each of his words.

"When you try to live a good and spiritual life, then the negative side works twice as hard to make sure that you don't, so you have to walk that fine line in-between. When you step on peoples' toes, then they try to dis your name, dis you as a person, and you have to deal with all that crap instead of taking care of your mom and the kids. You don't have to judge that, but you have to be aware of your environment. It's hard to do that sometimes. You think you can help, but you're not helping by even suggestion solutions, because unless the Creator puts it in their mind, then they don't want to hear it."

"How do I talk to them without stepping on their toes?"

"I know not to elaborate on anything greater than what they can think about in their mind," he said. "When you pass away, you don't pass away with the community. You pass away by yourself and with the Creator. The community, the earth, and everything around you is to benefit you and the Creator, but there comes a time when it's just you and the Creator."

Chapter 7
STARTING OVER

Leslie told me to take control of my career by publishing my book. The idea was liberating but also terrifying. The last time I did that was ten years ago, after I had lost my agent. She was the vice president of a literary agency in New York and shortly after the release of her memoir, she decided to leave the agency and continue writing from home while keeping a small list of clientele. Left with no representation, I didn't know where to turn. My manuscripts had already endured a dozen rejections and even though I had gone on to write more books, I did not have a single one published.

My previous teachers, Chip and Susan, listened to my dilemma and, staring at me knowingly, advised me to publish the books myself. Otherwise my manuscripts would sit on bookshelves and collect dust. I imagined a dingy dark room full of the manuscripts that I'd spent years writing, bleeding over. I'd cut off a hefty chunk of socializing, lost some friends, and remained single for a long time to dedicate myself to my work. To let my writings be a mere container of dust would be insane! But self-publishing carried a stigma and required a business mentality that I was clueless about.

Yet the war on Iraq had just occurred, and my books had a timely appeal. This was my opportunity to showcase stories that could dispel stereotypes and help the world better understand and appreciate the Iraqi culture. Further, writing these books would keep me from feeling useless in a time of war. I wanted to express my anti-war ideals with lovely, beautiful stories, so I published my first book, *The Feminine Art*.

The day a thousand copies were shipped to my house, I sat in the garage and stared at them. I held the hardcover, touching it softly and even smelling the perfume of freshly printed paper. The front cover was a picture of my now deceased sister, Basima, before she became ill, before her illness ate her elegance and splendor. On the cover, she's sprawled like a cat on a blanket of grass, a large radio beside her, near the house which my siblings remember with opulent nostalgia as *Beit al Sikek*. Along with her picture was another picture of dangling gold coins of Middle Eastern origin. I was now an author. My dream had come true, though not in the way I'd expected.

The amount of work and the costs required to run a publishing house astounded me. Not only would I have to hire a book designer and book formatter, but I would need to get endorsements and find a printer, a warehouse, a distributor, and the list went on and on. To top it off, I had just gotten engaged. I worked seven days a week, nearly forty hours, and in between, I had to prepare for the engagement ceremonies and the wedding as well as spend time with my fiancé and in-laws.

The *kilma*, which literary translates to word, is a pre-engagement ceremony where the future groom and his family come to the future bride's house. The girl stays in her room until the man's elders have made the official request for her hand in marriage, and then she's cued to appear. In my case, my husband's aunt poetically said to my mother, "We want to take a flower from your garden and put it in our garden."

My mother gave her approval, ululation followed, and I was asked to come downstairs where, in front of our closest family, my future fiancé presented me with a bouquet of flowers. He later also put a necklace around me that publicly confirmed I was spoken for.

The night before this gathering, I had stayed up until the early morning hours creating press kits for my books. I stuffed book after book into envelopes, labeled them, sealed them, and stamped them with the words "Media Mail." After placing an ad on Radio and Television Interview Report, I received constant calls from radio hosts wanting to interview me. I never said no, not even when I had class or work. I would wing it, going into the bathroom or sitting in my car or stepping outside in the parking lot to do the interviews using my cell phone even though the host had asked me to use a landline. Over a hundred interviews were done in this manner, and no one ever asked me much of anything about the book. They wanted to know about my childhood in Iraq, about what it was like to live under Saddam's regime in a Muslim country. The interviews often went for longer than initially scheduled because people kept calling in with questions or the host was intrigued by the stories I told.

During that time, I turned into an octopus with six arms and two legs in order to handle the tasks at hand: studying for film school, where I was a fulltime student; finding my engagement dress; choosing the floral designs and bridal cake for my wedding banquet; searching for the home we'd be living in and the furniture we needed to buy; and dealing with the drama that results from weddings when one relative feels offended that they were not invited to the henna party or the engagement party or whatever had offended them.

The day of my wedding, on the way home from the salon, I called my school to pay my monthly tuition. I normally mailed a check, but this time I had way too much to do and, worried it would be late, wanted to pay through credit card. The guy on the phone said I still could send it through mail, even if it arrived late.

"Well, I'm getting married today and leaving for my honeymoon early tomorrow morning, so I wouldn't be able to send it for another week at least," I said.

The guy was tongue-tied, probably at the extent of my practicality.

I ended up publishing my first two novels, the first one during my engagement period and the second one while I was pregnant with my first child. The process was a lot of work but immensely rewarding. While my books did not sell like hotcakes, I did receive awards from the community, recognition from the media, and jobs as a freelance writer and translator. But I was not looking for prestige. I wanted people to read the books.

I prayed that I would not have to take the self-publishing route again. Perhaps I could strengthen and refine my platform, self-publish my previous manuscripts which sat idly in my desk drawers, and then try, once again, to find an agent or a small traditional publisher. I had, by now, finished writing the first of the four-part memoir series. Maybe, after strengthening and refining my platform, I could sell that and then later find a home for *The Great American Family*.

I called a publicist for a free consultation. She examined my online presence and said there were a number of missing components that every successful author had to have: a website, an eBook version of their books, reviews on Amazon, a Facebook page, a Twitter account, a Google Plus, Tumblr, and other funky names. She told me that she would do me a disservice by charging me money to promote my work because I needed a total online makeover first. Basically, I was not ready to come out into the world.

I thanked her for her honesty and went online to see what the hell she was talking about. That was when it struck me. During the three years that I entered a cave, worked on my spirituality, had conversations with spirits, and wrote my heart out, I had fallen into the Stone Age. Technology had advanced. There were marketing terms I had never heard of. My online appearance was a hot mess. Now what?

I lit incense and knelt on the rug in my office. Facing the painting of a wolf, I closed my eyes and asked God why was it that every time I was ready to abandon this career, to feel free of this ongoing struggle, I ended up having to leap further into it. I wanted to let go of the intellectual life and to give myself up to other work. Maybe plant gardens, interact with the earth's soil, and grow crops that were visible and edible. Maybe teach children. But was that feasible? Once someone receives a calling, is there an escape? And why didn't a calling come with considerable gifts and strengths? Why didn't the process happen easily and naturally and come with a long list of volunteers?

I recalled the story of Jonah, who was swallowed by a whale after he avoided God's calling to head to Nineveh and forewarn them that their city would be overthrown in forty days if they did not forsake their cruel and violent lifestyle. Jonah did not want to go to that dreadful, sinful city, so he said to God, "I know you too well, O God. If anybody, by repenting, gives you half a chance to be merciful, you'll change your mind and won't carry out your sentence upon them." Then he fled to Tarshish. Eventually Jonah did follow his path. He went to Nineveh and delivered the message to its people. They listened. The king of Nineveh proclaimed a fast and declared that every one of his citizens would abandon their evil and violent ways and cry mightily to God. They did so, and the city was spared.

In his book, *Success is a Calling!* Ashbel Vudzijena writes, "Most people avoid their calling, but when you avoid the calling you are denying yourself the miraculous guidance of God." He writes that avoiding God's calling causes disappointment and stress in one's life.

Storytelling was my calling, my garden. The words I planted into each page created the crops that fed my soul and those around me, even if they did not read the pages. I surrendered to this truth, and by the time I stood to my feet and walked off the rug, I knew what I had to do to clean up my literary mess.

Chapter 8
FAMILY CONSTELLATION

The woman that headed my writing group, Mary, invited me to accompany her to a lecture series hosted by the Metropolitan Detroit A.R.E. (Association of Research and Enlightenment) Community, a nonprofit organization which was founded in 1931 by Edgar Cayce. Cayce was an American Christian mystic who connected with the universal consciousness and from this state answered questions on various subjects, such as healing, reincarnation, wars, and future events. A biographer gave him the nickname "The Sleeping Prophet."

The subject at the A.R.E. meeting was Family Constellations, and two men described how unconscious limits to success often stem initially from the unresolved and many times unspoken traumas, tragedies, and transgressions that weave themselves into the energy, fabric, and conversations of our family. The men offer workshops to help people detox from family pain or drama.

"We hold many of our histories in our bodies, in our flesh," said Robert Auerback, one of the speakers. "Family Constellations is a different way to heal resistant, stubborn patterns that might not be ours, or it might be an issue that goes back into past family generation trauma or transgressions that was never healed or resolved. This energy sticks from generation to generation because it's an unconscious process."

"It's done without making anyone wrong, or putting blame on anyone," said Vince Anthony Pitre, the other speaker. "It's about seeing where issues came from so we can find a resolution. You don't heal by chasing light all day. You have to face the dark side as well."

Through movement and unspoken words, people in the room get psychologically reconfigured. Not only is the person with the problem being healed but so are their family members, even if they are not in the room.

"In this process, new images come up that counters what the person thought of themselves growing up," Pitre said. "The person leaves behind their old story. This allows their brain to rewire to this new image, which they step into, and then they are able to move on with their life."

Bert Hellinger founded this therapeutic method, Family Constellations, which draws on elements of family systems therapy, existential phenomenology, and Zulu attitudes to family. Hellinger was a priest whose travels to Africa led to his fascination with how the natives honored their ancestors and the way in which they helped each other heal.

Vince's office was in my area. I loved that this type of healing was growing to such an extent that a person could find someone that practiced it in local cities. For years, I had believed that holistic health was going to become as popular as yoga classes, and now I saw it happening. Such workshops, teachings, and healings were especially beneficial for those who grew up in old tribal mentalities that limit them from their full potential.

I scheduled a consultation with Vince, arrived at my one o'clock appointed time, and enjoyed a cup of orange-flavored tea as I sat in the reception area. Native American flute music played in the background, the kind that Chip and Susan used to play at their house, especially during lab night when someone volunteered to hop on the massage table and we performed Reiki on him or her.

Vince, a man in his mid-to-late forties, came out and escorted me to his office. He was a comely man with a shaven head and a gentle smile, a bit on the thin side and not too tall. I placed my purse on the floor, handed him my coat to hang on the door, and sat down in a wide leather chair. He sat across from me, a small table between us. He asked me what I wanted from this session, and I said, "I want to meet the right people who will accept, publish, and promote my work and help it become a success."

I told him how, for years, the pattern had been that I connect with well-reputable people. The project, whether a book or feature script, would get very close to getting executed, and then it never came full circle. It wasn't the quality of my work, because people easily came on board, wanting to represent me or partner with me.

"They saw the gift," he said.

"Yes. They not only believed in my work, but they knew it would be profitable. When things did not go as planned, I continued to produce work, knowing that one day things would change. I spent over four years on a manuscript that I acquired an agent for, but last year I fired her because her personal life was interfering with her business. I have arrived where I am today pretty much on my own, but I can't do that anymore. At this point, for my career to get to the next level, I must team up with the right people to get it where it needs to go."

"So you're always getting this close," he said, pinching his fingers, "this close, but then it doesn't happen."

"Exactly, and I don't know what it is, but I want to make sure that I'm not somehow blocking the process because of fear or other negative vibes. When I talked to Lynn Andrews, my teacher, about this, she said it seemed that I'm sabotaging my success and that I needed to get out of my own way. The problem is, I don't know how I'm sabotaging it."

"Or whether the part that's sabotaging it was inherited from your family, from generations ago," he said. "Memories are passed down through generations in our DNA."

"I had recently learned about that."

A 2013 research study from Emory University School of Medicine in Atlanta showed that it is possible for some information to be inherited biologically through chemical changes that occur in DNA. Scientists applied electric shocks to mice as they exposed them to the smell of cherry blossoms. The mice then bred, and both the children and grandchildren of the affected rodents demonstrated a fear of cherry blossoms the first time they smelled them.

According to the *Telegraph*, Dr. Brian Dias from the department of psychiatry at Emory University said, "From a translational perspective, our results allow us to appreciate how the experiences of a parent, before even conceiving offspring, markedly influence both structure and function in the nervous system of subsequent generations. Such a phenomenon may contribute to the etiology and potential intergenerational transmission of risk for neuropsychiatric disorders such as phobias, anxiety, and post-traumatic stress disorder."

"So let me first ask you, what are you afraid of?" Vince asked.

I thought about that. "I'm afraid that what I say in my books will upset people, that as an Iraqi-American woman, I don't have the right to express my political views the way an average American has, even though what I say has a greater value because I have seen both sides of the truth. In the past, I noticed that people were offended by me saying I had a happy childhood in Iraq. It contradicted their perception of Iraq being this murky, dangerous place. They tried to shut me out, dismiss what I had to say, and in a way, I recoiled. When it came time to write *The Great American Family*, I noticed that I had lost my literary voice. There was so much inside me that needed to be told, but my past experiences stifled me. Lynn's school healed the wounds that prevented me from writing. The mentors and assignments empowered me to where I wrote the book in a most honest and powerful way. Now that I'm looking for a home for it, the fear of people preventing me from doing that is popping up again."

"You know that what we oppose, we project," he said. "If someone priced his book at thirty-five dollars but felt that this price is too high and people will not think it's worth thirty-five dollars, then when someone looks at the price of that book, they'll think, 'this price is too high. It's not worth thirty-five dollars.' The rejections are a mirror of what you're projecting in the universe."

He's right, I thought. The universe smells my fear and throws it back at me.

"You are a powerful writer," he said. "When I read that post you wrote about Family Constellations, and some other things you wrote, I thought, this is a powerful writer who will make a great impact through her writing." Then he said, "So let's look at your family history here and see what may be preventing your work from moving forward. I read what you wrote in the questionnaire about your dad and how he lost the house and had bad business tactics."

"He was a very gifted and hard-working man who failed to provide well for his family because he allowed others to take advantage of him. I know I'm not like that, that I manage things pretty well and I don't let opportunities slip away. But the pattern of getting so close to having something and it not coming full circle reminds me of how that house he built was only a thousand dinars shy of completion and we lost it. It could have changed our whole life."

"What about your mother? Tell me about her."

"My mother was twelve years old when she married my father. She had twelve kids and she basically devoted her life to her home and her family and raised us to be the same way. All of the women from my mother's tribe are known to be very good with holding a family together. From my mother's side, women rarely divorce. They manage their home like a millionaire manages his company. Those who marry difficult men end up straightening them out, and if he was poor when they married him, he ends up prospering thanks to her."

"So the abundance came from your mother?"

"I supposes, yes," I said, never having thought of it that way, and remembered a story my maternal aunt had told me recently about how much my grandfather had loved my grandmother. He had cried so much for her after she passed away, my aunt had never imagined anyone had this much tears in them. "My mother was never heard, you know. When we laughed at her remarks, she always said, 'you're just like your father. He didn't take what I had to say seriously.'"

"He missed out on listening to what she had to say."

I imagined how much stronger and wealthier our family would have been had he listened to her rather than all those people who had repeatedly taken advantage of him.

"I want to change my story," I said. "I feel that the rejections of the past have weighed heavily on me. Those rejections are no longer my truth, and I want to get over them. Maybe I took these rejections so hard because I come from a culture where you're supposed to be impeccable, and that's the case especially for women. Women carry the weight of bringing honor or shame to their family."

"That's a lot of responsibility, and they're not even rewarded for it."

I laughed. I thought, how hard the women in my family have worked, in their home, outside of their home, in their community. Yet, because they were not used to rewarding themselves, they skipped the reward and did not know why they felt tired and frustrated.

"There are a lot of directions we can go here," he said, looking at the notebook in his hand where he'd scribbled a bunch of notes. He scanned the paper. "One word that you kept mentioning is rejection." He counted the numbers. "You said it four times."

"In the first school year, we were to make an altar and place the things that we wanted to get rid of on the death side. I placed all my rejection letters there because I wanted that part of my life to be over. I want a new story."

"Who was the most rejected in your family?"

"My father was a Christian man in a Muslim-dominated country and he would not join the Baath Party, so that disabled him from having certain rights or getting ahead in his work. He used to be an outspoken man, and that got him into trouble a couple of times. So in my birth country, our religion and non-political associations was somewhat of an issue. Here in the United States, our Iraqi background held us back in other ways. And I was rejected a lot with my work as well as in personal relationships. When my relationships didn't work out, I assumed there was something wrong with me or it was my fault because I wasn't your average Chaldean girl. I didn't know any girl who shared the same interests as I did."

He continued to look over his notes.

"I feel that this book has to be birthed into the world," I said. "It's overdue. It's like a pregnant woman carrying a baby for longer than its term. If the baby is not born, one of two things happens – either she dies, or the baby dies."

"How far would you go for your work?" he asked, staring into my eyes with a smile. "Would you die for it?"

His question jolted me. I immediately imagined my children without a mother. "I'm not afraid to die," I said, and then, my lips quivering, I added, "But my family…" Tears came down my face. "I don't want any harm to come to them as a result of my work. And if I die, what would happen to them?"

"So we hit something here," he said.

My fear for the welfare of my family had subconsciously prevented me from releasing this project, *The Great American Family*, into the universe with love and confidence.

"I discussed this project with my husband before I took it on. I told him I was afraid, and he said to do it for God. I finally accepted because the story kept stalking me, eating at my conscience, and I knew that doing the right thing would be a blessing for my family the way my ancestors' good deeds have been a blessing for us. But now that it's ready to fly, I am holding on somehow. I don't know what to expect."

He looked at an area at my lower right and said, "What time do you have to leave?"

"I have to be out of here by three o'clock to go pick up my kids from school."

"I'm going to go check my schedule at the desk. If I don't have another appointment, I'm going to spend a little more time with you. I won't charge you for that. I just feel there's a lot of things going on here, and I want our work together to be able to help you."

When he returned, he asked me to pull the handle on the side of the chair so I could lay back. I placed my feet on the foot stool and crossed them.

"It's better that you uncross your ankles, because the energy will better run through you," he said.

I uncrossed my ankles, closed my eyes, and listened to the meditative music he had on. He asked me to take several deep, long breaths and relax. He used a large flute-like instrument to blow wind, and it reminded me of when my Native American teacher played his flute.

"I know you've been doing a lot of school work and assignments, but you need to allow," he said. "Allow energy to flow through you."

I released the need to focus and work hard to get things done. As my breathing and heartbeat slowed down, bright colored flowers appeared, moving and floating in 3-D, their pedals dancing softly and exotically. The most dominant color was pistachio, but there were also pinks and yellows. Their splendor took my breath away.

"I want you to look at your life and see all that has happened that brought you here to this moment," he said.

I saw my birth, my childhood, my arrival to America, my struggles and pains, my joys and triumphs.

"Now imagine your father standing behind you, on the

right side." He paused. "Imagine your mother standing behind you, to the left side. Now imagine your father's parents standing behind him and your mother's parents standing behind her, even if you have never seen them before. Now imagine your father's grandparents standing behind him and your mother's grandparents standing behind her, and so on and so forth until eternity."

One by one their spirits appeared and created a golden aura and an extremely warm and peaceful environment.

"I want you to symbolically turn around and face them, see your parents and grandparents and your ancestors who have brought you to this moment," he said.

I did so and in their eyes, their clothes, the texture of their skin, I saw their strength and goodness and smelled the scent of our once heavenly ancestral village, now ravaged by barbarism.

"They are proud of you, and they support you fully," he said. "Thank and honor them for the work they have done before you, which brought you to where you are today."

He continued to say things about my ancestors, and I went further and further into the meditation until a bright, gorgeous light surrounded me and replaced the flowing flowers. Then he said, "I want you to give me your left hand." He held my hand. "I want you to remember the first time you felt you were not standing in your own power."

I frowned as an image appeared of that day in Baghdad when the principle slapped me in front of the whole school.

"How old were you?" he asked.

"Seven or eight."

"I want you to see who was there and what everyone was doing when this happened."

The sun shined brightly. The school courtyard had hundreds

of children lined up. I was called to the front of the line. When I got there, the principal looked down on me with the most loathing eyes and mean, red-painted lips. She lifted her hand high, and I do not remember the pain of the actual slap. The shock of it all caused me to pass out. When I opened my eyes, I was in the classroom looking at my teacher and the students who were comforting me.

Tears rushed down my face. I thought this incident was far behind me, but punishing me like that in front of the entire school at such a young age when no one had laid a hand on me before had caused much more harm than I'd realized. I remembered Lynn's words. She often said that those who are abused as children avoid shining in the world because they are afraid that someone will hurt or punish them. Now I understood what she meant.

"I want you to hold that seven-year-old girl and comfort her in the way that she might not have been comforted at that time," he said.

I held and hugged her the way I would my daughter and told her it was not her fault that her government was an asshole. I told her she had done nothing wrong, and that the day she was slapped for doing nothing wrong caused her for decades to doubt herself even when she was doing a good thing. She believed that she would get slapped no matter what, and so time and time again, doors were shut on her. She kept projecting those slaps.

Suddenly I saw myself pulling her by the arm to rescue her out of that land. I ran, and the energy of my parents sacrificing everything to get us out of Iraq and into America penetrated my body. The painting that Chip had once given me flashed before my eyes, of the woman holding a baby and walking away from burning oil fields. "She's leaving her birth country and walking toward democracy," he had said to me.

I finally understood what he had meant. For days I had been thinking about this painting. Toward the end of last year, I brought it up from the basement and placed it in my office. Recently I wanted to do a ceremony in front of it, to understand the message Chip was giving me. It was an inappropriate wedding gift, but now it was starting to make sense. I finally embraced it as I saw myself doing whatever I could to get this little girl out of that godforsaken country.

The face of Saddam suddenly surfaced, accompanied with words of apology. He apologized for having triggered so much fear inside of me, for causing the type of harm that helped bring the country of Iraq to ruins. He said, "Forget about me. I am no longer here. Forget the past. It's no longer a part of you."

His image began to dissipate, and I realized I needed to disconnect from the past and my birth country, that I could still love it and remember it without the attachment that held me back from completely enjoying the freedoms of my new country.

Vince guided me to release whatever I needed to release from that incident, occasionally using the big flute to blow several deep breaths. He said, "I want you to see a door and walk through it."

A majestic garden door emerged.

"I want you to walk through that door and see your future."

I stepped through it and into the islands of Greece and the picturesque towns I'd been to in Europe. I relived the feeling I had when I traveled, with no worries about writing or my writing career. I was free, not connected to my past and not caring about my future. I'd just wanted to have fun.

He blessed my future, said that as it blossomed, it would

happen with safety and protection. At those words, I took a deep breath to secure the blessings. He rang a soft sounding bell and sprinkled herbal spray over my head, which lifted my spirit to a blissful state. Each sound and fragrance washed away whatever threads lingered from my past and further drove me into the potion of my future. He said he was going to give me time to spend in my future and left the room. The future expanded, as if an additional secret passage had been unlocked and made available. Soon afterward I was connected to other parts of the world, other planets and even the stars. The light increased and my journey went farther and farther, so much so that when Vince said that I could open my eyes when I was ready, I had great difficulty doing so.

"I traveled very very far," I said when I finally was able to open my eyes.

"For the next three days, the space will be available for you to continue dreaming your new future into your reality."

Chapter 9

BECOMING FULLY RAINBOW

"The amount of intent you put into this school is the amount you will get out of it," I often heard my mentors and Lynn say. I decided to burn all bridges and never go back to where I once was career-wise. The rainbow inside of me wanted to shine, wanted its spectrum of lights to appear in the sky and not be buried behind a fog of nurturing duties. I had played the role of nurturer since the age of twelve, with nieces and nephews and now with my children and my mother. I had served my tribe, and now I wanted to let go and form a multicolored arc near the sun, to be a fulltime rainbow.

Lynn said not to quit as we neared the finish line, and I wasn't about to quit. While technology had taken me out of the loop for too long, it also brought good news. Nowadays, publishing was a cinch in comparison to when I'd published my first two books, and it was free. There was something called CreateSpace and a load of services available at my fingertips. There were many authors who had taken their literary careers into their own hands and succeeded. Amanda Hocking wrote seventeen novels in her free time. She couldn't find a traditional publisher, so she published them herself as eBooks, selling over a million copies and earning two million from sales. She ended up receiving a seven-figure advance from St. Martin's Press for her work.

Most authors who had self-published and succeeded wrote romance, horror, sci-fi, or young adult novels. Some wrote motivational books, health books, etc. My books did not fall into these categories. They were more literary. Doubts entered my mind until one day, while reading a book about Jane Austen's life, I learned that she'd self-published her novels after a long-winded, difficult, and unprofitable interaction with a publisher. She'd even edited her own work. Virginia Woolf, Ezra Pound, Thomas Paine, Beatrix Potter, and other revolutionary authors believed in themselves enough to invest in their work and make their dreams come true.

"Publish your books," Leslie said to me at the end of last year. "Don't depend on anyone else to do it."

I found an affordable editor, book designer, and book formatter, pulled my first two novels from out of the gutters, revised them, polished them up, and republished them as a new edition. My third novel then received the same treatment. I gathered my poems, which were published in publications around the world, and put them inside one poetry book. I did all of this in a matter of months, and it was quite painful. I sat behind my computer for so long that my body ached and I gained weight. I felt heavy and sluggish, but the words would not stop pouring out of my fingertips.

* * *

The next time the apprentices had a call with Lynn was during the month of March. I asked her, "I often encounter family members who ask me to take on nurturing tasks that I'm trying to lessen the amount of in my life. I've learned to say no and set boundaries, but sometimes I still feel guilty and frustrated by their desire for me to nurture them. This year especially, I feel my Rainbow energy is flourishing, so I'd like to end this pattern. I'm just not sure what's attracting this type of attention."

"You've got to remember that you've become a bright light in your life, and people are drawn to you like a moth to a flame. All you can do with dignity and grace and much love is say, you know, if I'm to put everything that I am to my practice, there are some things I have to say no to, and I have to put boundaries for myself so that I don't infringe on decisions that I already made."

I was not quite satisfied with that answer and tried to better explain my dilemma. People attracted to this teaching came to the council, but then they expected me to share what I've learned in the manner they expected me to share it. They wanted me to be nurturing because they were used to me being a nurturer, but I no longer wanted to be everyone's nurturer. They were family, so our relationship was well-established, and it was hard to change roles. Lynn had no answer for me and asked my mentor her opinion on this subject. My mentor incorporated her thoughts and then Lynn said a few words and jumped to the next question.

Lynn sometimes turns into a *heyoka*, but one has to be tuned in enough to recognize what she's doing, though oftentimes it comes so natural to her that she doesn't know she's doing it. A heyoka is a kind of sacred clown in the culture of the Lakota people. He speaks, moves, and reacts in an opposite fashion to the people around them. The sacred clown aims to deflate the ego by reminding those in power of their own shortcomings. They also remind those who are not in power that power has the likelihood to corrupt if taken too seriously. It must be balanced with other forces, such as humor, so that we don't see ourselves as enlightened masters when in actuality we might be spiritually naïve.

Later, in response to another apprentice's question about power, she said, "When you search for power, power starts taking a look at you and wonders if you're really strong enough to handle what's coming. In other words, are you strong enough to be a powerful woman or a dangerous woman? That means getting to a place where nobody is going to fool with you because they sense that steel bar down your backbone. You're not going to be pushed around, go past your boundaries, and you do not allow anyone to step into your circle of power unless they're asked to come. People sense it. You don't have to say anything."

Her reaction to my question, coupled with this answer, caused me to examine my own animosities and weaknesses. She wanted to prevent me from taking myself too seriously or believing that I am more powerful than I am.

"When you're confronted with a situation that you're not quite sure of, you move into that place of power that you know you have, into your body-mind, and you ask, is this a petty tyrant?" Lynn said. "A petty tyrant is someone who's testing you. Someone who upsets you is perhaps your best teacher. They make you grow because you have to look at why you're upset at them. How do they have the power to upset you? And learn to stalk the answers to these things. You stalk the petty tyrant and look at it. A shaman is someone who choreographs energy in the world."

Another caller wanted to know what the difference was between working with our energies versus working with the luminous fibers. Lynn said that there was a very fine line between the two. The energy that you feel is life force. Life force then empowers the luminous fibers. The luminous fibers are the energy strings of life that go around you and help you keep your form in the relative world, this existence, then they move out into the world to connect to other luminous fibers. Luminous fibers create a matrix around the whole earth, so we affect each other in an exquisite way.

She said that life force was a different thing. "It's how you see that life force coming to you. It's your life," she said. "It's how you wake up in the morning, what you do with your day and your thoughts. What you think every single day is what is feeding and forming your cellular system. Are you thinking light, ways to become more powerful, better, kinder, more grateful in the world, or are you complaining and full of tears and terror and negative aspects?"

She talked about the luminous fibers in wars, during explosions, and how they impacted the earth. She mentioned an article she read in *National Geographic* entitled "How Art Heals the Wounds of War." One retired marine, who had been exposed to more than 300 explosions, said that most of his injuries are invisible and the rest hidden. Chip and Susan, I remembered, had taught their students that thoughts and actions are like stones dropped in a pond, creating a ripple that travels outward.

Nancy asked about the place where we would be graduating, and Lynn said it was a fabulous place in Scottsdale. You fly into Phoenix, and it's about a twenty minute drive to the Franciscan Renewal Center, twenty-four acres right in the midst of the most elegant part of town. Once you're there, you realize you're in the wilderness. There's a pool, a church, a chapel, a lawn with big trees, fountains, and majestic camelback mountains booming right over you. It is very respectful, peaceful, and rejuvenating.

"It's kind of like being in a tribe," she said and added that this was our last year. "But remember, the end is always the beginning."

I looked forward to graduating this year and going out into the world. I'd had enough of being a student who hopped from one learning institute to another. I was also tired of finding ugly and unpleasant aspects of myself and others.

"Once the school is completed, the pressure is off," Nancy said. "And you can do whatever you want to do with what you learned."

Chapter 10
A YEAR OF COMPLETION

"Why do I and the other apprentices feel like this year, we're being pulled in different directions?" I asked Nancy.

"The fourth year of school is a year of completion," Nancy said. "The first few years you hold things to your heart. You are not really ready to share them yet. Now the circle is getting bigger, and the teachings are incorporated in every part of your life. Even after you leave the school, you will see the circle get bigger, and while life gets more complicated, it also becomes simpler. It really all fits together. It's all part of the polarity. All the experiences we have, have polar opposites."

I asked her about the feminine and masculine shields.

"Oftentimes creative people carry a strong feminine side," she said. "Male jobs, like car race driving, have a strong masculine shield. Someone who struggles in life financially has a weak feminine shield. A strong feminine shield says, 'No, you're not going to take that food from my children.' A weak feminine shield will say, 'Go ahead and take that food because I love you.' A wounded person can sabotage themselves. Any wounded person has to heal to get to their optimum level. It's important to have the male and female shield balance each other out."

"I assumed the feminine shield is submissive," I said. "In

my culture, I come off as strong or even angry when I express myself because certain emotions which I hold back in consideration of this and that person suddenly explode."

"You need to become the goddess within yourself," she said. "The goddess experienced a suppressed journey through the patriarchal world. I did not used to stand up for myself because my mom was like that with my father. Lynn helped me find the goddess within myself. Those goddesses were reflective of societies that held them in great esteem. Just by holding that within yourself, your confidence will flourish. The world needs for the goddess to stand up. They used to stand up for forests. They stood up for communities. They stood up for children. Over time these goddesses were taken down and replaced by the gods. What the goddess wants more than anything in the world is peace in the world and peace between everyone.

"This is a worldwide women rebirthing. We all share it. It's very important for women to be strong now. They've been made to feel less important. We're all missing out in this process. Even the men miss out. It takes a very strong man to live with a strong woman. Some men are afraid of strong women, and some women are afraid of their own strengths."

In Unraveling the Mysteries of Ancient Places, Margaret Moose writes a chapter about Jezebel and the biblical conflict in Samaria, an ancient city which today is split between Israeli and Palestinian control. In the bible, Samaria was condemned by the Hebrew prophets for its ivory houses and luxurious palaces displaying pagan riches. But Moose contends that it is the worship of a female deity that was the deepest issue in this conflict. This is when Jezebel, the wife of King Ahab in the kingdom of Israel, came along with her own religious beliefs, which interfered with the exclusive worship of the Hebrew god Yahweh. Because she spoke her mind and stood behind her beliefs and culture, she was viewed as dangerous and came to be known as an archetype of the wicked woman and the hated harlot. Consequently, writes Moose, the goddess was removed from the [biblical] story as much as possible to hide the fact of her once widespread power. The presence of the female in the divine was simply an unthinkable state to the followers of Yahweh at this time, as it is to the three Yahweh-based religions.

In an interview with Bill Moyers, Joseph Campbell stated that the Great Goddess "was associated primarily with agriculture and the agricultural societies. It has to do with the earth. The human woman gives birth just as the earth gives birth to the plants…so woman magic and earth magic are the same. They are related. And the personification of the energy that gives birth to forms and nourishes forms is properly female. It is in the agricultural world of ancient Mesopotamia, the Egyptian Nile, and in the earlier planting-culture systems that the Goddess is the dominant mythic form."

Campbell argues that Christianity, originally a denomination of Judaism, embraced part of the Jewish pagan culture. The rib metaphor is an example of how distant the Jewish religion was from the prehistoric religion, the worship of the Goddess.

Leslie called me on a Sunday morning in early March.

"I had a dream about you," she said. "There was a large gathering, with women dancing and celebrating. There was a teenager. I don't know whether it was you or someone else. I went up to her, gave her a rose and placed a three-quarter sleeve shall on her. The three-quarter shall is important not only on a personal level, but on a spiritual level."

I was getting ready to go to church and asked her if we

could reconnect during the week because I wanted to talk to her about several things. We agreed to talk Tuesday night and hung up. That Sunday, *The Flavor of Cultures*, my third novel, was published on Amazon and Kindle. That same week it was made available at Barnes & Noble and through other distributors, some of which included libraries. It was a wonderful feeling to see it come alive. Now that it had wings, it could fly. God only knows where it would fly to. The possibilities were so exciting.

"I've written three manuscripts since the school started," I told Leslie the next time we talked.

"Is that all?"

We both laughed, but her words triggered a nerve. She knew I could do better than that.

I told her the story of Maria Theresa Asmar, a woman born in Telkaif in 1804, the birth village of my parents and grandparents. During her time, Iraq, then called Mesopotamia, was occupied by the Ottoman Empire. As a young woman, Maria traveled to Europe by herself and met prominent people, including Queen Victoria. Queen Victoria ended up sponsoring Maria's work, a memoir which amounted to 720 pages.

The Chaldean community gave little recognition to this work evidently, because I and most others had never heard of it. In 2012, I covered a story where a British-Iraqi woman came to the United States and gave a lecture regarding this book. As I listened to the British woman speak, I thought of how reading this book could have dramatically influenced my life. She and I had so many similarities, though she was born nearly 200 years before me.

"I want you to look at that woman and tell me how she mirrors you," Leslie said.

Maria and I were both Christian women born and raised in

a Muslim country. She traveled alone to Europe. She met with higher ups, and she was a prolific writer. The difference was that she had financial support from Queen Victoria whereas I have not attained that type of financial support, although that's not entirely true because my husband works and supports our home and prior to that, my brothers supported our home.

"She surrendered her power to the queen, but you did not have to do that," Leslie said. "You fulfilled your karmic payback. This time you did not have to give away your power."

This time? I had goosebumps.

"Yes, I have goosebumps too," Leslie said, although I didn't say a word about my goosebumps. "You see her energy very clearly, and the things she had to do at that time to get where she needed to get. She was fearless, although the world was not ready to hear her then. Here you are again. The world is too full of fears on many levels and is not ready to hear you. You're finishing the work she started two centuries ago."

I couldn't speak.

"I still have goosebumps, so I know I'm right," she said. "You've now seen one of your past lives. Now you can acknowledge her and pull in her energy. Place the book she wrote on the life side of your altar." She paused, yelled at the barking dog that kept demanding her attention, then resumed. "You were talking about Jane Austen. This was the same time period. I'm wondering if the other author, Maria, had ever been friends with Jane Austen and it's a style you're comfortable with."

Earlier I had told her how my previous literary agent and an Iraqi literature critic had both compared my style to that of Jane Austen.

I thanked her for the ability to understand my career struggles. Her advice and wisdom ran in my ears for years. She had connected with me on a cultural level, to my family and tribal dynamics, and I felt that she and I had a special mission.

"I take my work very seriously," she said. "Because we've built a relationship, we've shared a lifetime somewhere, and I'm supposed to help you remember. That's my job. It's about love. You're like my little sister, and big sisters protect their little sisters." Then she added, "I'm glad you found the messages in what I've told you and used them to your advantage."

I went back to Maria, the memoirist, and asked her what she saw that made her say what she said about us.

"Immediately I made the connection," she said. "You've made the same mistakes and the same leaps."

"You know, when I turned in the article about Maria to my editor, she said that maybe I was Maria reincarnated, with a question mark."

"That was talking to her, and she probably didn't know why."

"I immediately felt that yes, I easily could be. Then I forgot all about Maria."

"You're too close. You couldn't see it. That's what the school is about, remembering who you are and pulling from that energy. Put her picture and her book on the life force of the altar."

She told me she was going to stop mentoring next year. After that, she was considering visiting me in Michigan. I was ecstatic and asked if she would stay with me. She said she could.

"I've been here to keep you in the school, to keep you in from A-to-Z without all the history and the drama," she said. "I understand why Lynn didn't put you in the writing school. She put you in the Mystery school because you had to take your power back, to be who you are and to know how to use the tools and share the tools with your kids so that it's not just handed from father to son but mother to daughter. It's slicing cake and seeing who you'll give it to. All the knowledge is the cake. It's sharing of the knowledge and helping others to remember."

Before we hung up, she said she wanted me to put a board on the refrigerator where I added gold stars each time my children accomplished something good. I thanked her for this suggestion because lately I had felt overwhelmed and therefore unable to focus on their accomplishments rather than their shortcomings.

"You're Type-A personality," she said. "So am I. We kick ass and take shit later. You work yourself into a frenzy. You keep asking, what's after this? What's after that? As if you're in a factory. This type of personality helps people move forward rather than being stuck, but you're swirling in a tornado. Be the center of the tornado and as things are going around, give yourself closure. We have a tendency to take something really simple and make it complicated. Also, remember to celebrate your accomplishments."

"I still fall short with that. Like the other day, I was excited to celebrate the publication of my book, and then time passed and I forgot to do anything and I was on to the next task on my to-do list. I have a number of projects I had not completed to the fullest before and now I'm ready to complete them, but I feel overwhelmed."

"But honey, you're worth finishing these projects. You're a multi-faceted jewel and in order to shine, you have to be polished. Give yourself permission to do one thing at a time."

Chapter 11
WORTHY OF THE FINISH LINE

I tried to take a nap when my daughter walked in and asked if she could paint her nails. I did not open my eyes, cueing for her to leave. She asked again and again. Then she came and put her arms around me and asked, "Mom, can I do my nails?"

"You woke me up for that?" I asked.

She stomped out of the room. I couldn't believe the lack of consideration, the absolute carelessness, the…my eyes fell on the clock, which read 4:07 pm. I had a scheduled call with Nancy! I hurried out of bed and grabbed my phone. "I forgot we were supposed to talk today even though earlier in the day I knew about it," I told her.

I described my day's events, explaining how I'd taken care of my children's needs, my mother's needs, my husband's needs, my home's needs.

"It sounds like there's a lot going on," she said. "Living in the now is the way to live *now*. Also give yourself a lot of love. I can't stand when people say 'just relax,' but it's true. You give, give, give and you don't give enough to yourself. It's wonderful because you're so giving. Give yourself credit for that. It's wonderful for the people that are receiving your love and compassion, but as soon as it changes from a good feeling to a bad feeling, you need to put a stop to it and give yourself love. Be aware of that. Keep a chart and see how much you give and how much you receive."

She told me a story about when she went to Lynn's gathering for the first time. She was pouring so much love around her, love to people, love to nature, just wanting to heal everything and everyone that someone came and said to her, "Save some for yourself."

"You're Rainbow?" Nancy asked.

"I'm Rainbow with a very nurturing mother. At first, I thought I could be both. Then after looking further into it and having a long talk with Leslie, I realized how Rainbow was at the core of my heart and nurturing was what I learned from my mother and my culture. Trying to fit into a nurturing role had drained me, and little by little I began to let go of it. Yet I had to maintain an orderly lifestyle because that's what I grew up with and I work best in an organized environment. I found creative ways to enjoy the nurturing part of myself. I loved it, but for a while, I've felt burdened by the enormous obligations: the house and kids, my work, my mom, the school work. When I published my book last week, I felt an excitement I had not expected to feel. Suddenly the feeling I had in the beginning of the year that I should quit my writing career changed to the opposite, that I should produce more work. The reason I had initially wanted to quit was because I was tired of feeling stuck in the north, the Spirit, and not arriving to the south, the physical."

"I love what you're saying about flourishing as a Rainbow, wanting to honor and embrace that. It's a strange cycle to be in. Trying to divide your time like that can get confusing. I just learned to walk away, to delegate things. For me, when I am unhappy with a situation, I get emotional – angry, bitter, or I feel sorry for myself. Go around the wheel and see where are you getting drained. Gratitude is an excellent way to dissipate negative energy. This pattern is part of the healing. If we continue to work on it, you will find that you're working on that same issue on a deeper level."

"If I could live twenty-four hours as Rainbow, I would be a much happier person and more beneficial to everyone around me."

"Imagine what life would be like if we lived every moment with happiness and vitality. It doesn't mean life will be easy. But living life to the fullest is what gives us the life we crave. Change is the only constant. I love that statement. Lots of people clutch to the past and are afraid of change. Oh, when I was sixteen, life was so nice, they'll say, and they hang onto that by trying to keep the same lifestyle, even the same hair. You can see the sadness and stagnation. The more we live consciously, the more skilled we are at finding this happiness, to soar with the joy of life. But first and foremost, you have to celebrate the publication of your book. Go out and eat wonderful food!"

She reminded me that today is a new moon and said Lynn wanted us to do an act of power for the year.

"List the things you need to let go of," she said. "It could be simple, like taking care of the many details that don't make you happy. Jot down the things that you want to accomplish by this time next year. This is a symbolic awareness of what you want to let go of and what you want to accomplish."

After I hung up, I was anxious to leave the house, get to a bookstore, and write my act of power. The whole time I was talking to Nancy, my son had wrestled with me on the bed, pulling my hand when I tried to take notes, pulling my arm so that I could not hold the telephone against my ear. He climbed on my back, talked into my available ear, did all sorts of other things to take my concentration away from the phone and focus it on him.

My sister told me she would be coming to visit my mom. I waited for her to arrive, then rushed out of the house, drove to Barnes & Noble, ordered a white chocolate mocha and started writing my act of power, which was to organize, prepare, write, publish/produce, and promote all the projects which I have left incompleted or have neglected. I would declutter, clean, and clear, as well as give birth to my old projects in order to make room for the new projects to bloom. The list was long and required a lot of details, but I knew that if I managed my time efficiently, took it one step at a time and rewarded myself appropriately, I could and would do it all and even absolutely love the process.

Chapter 12
I Authenticate Myself

My family packed our stuff into the minivan and, along with my brother's family, left the house at 9 am and headed up north to Suttons Bay. The warmth of spring and the scenery of trees, farms, lakes, and barns made the four-hour ride feel short and sweet. I brought along Jack Canfield's *The Success Principle*. I shared with the kids the first principle, which talks about taking a hundred percent accountability for your life. The second principle is finding your life purpose.

"My life purpose is to be a teacher," my daughter said.

"You want to teach children or adults?" I asked.

"Children. Adults are crazy."

"Why is that?"

"They get more and more friends as they get older, and they have crazy conversations."

Wonder where she got that idea from, I thought, remembering the Ancient Wisdom Council meeting that blew up from its preliminary Zen atmosphere. During a follow-up council meeting, I proposed we use the talking stick. Whoever held the stick could express their point of view without anyone else interrupting. When finished, she would pass the stick to the next person. Everyone nodded in agreement, their impatient eyes ready to leap and snatch the stick. The oldest sister got the first turn, and then the turns became mumbo jumbo as various hands reached for the stick when the person was not done speaking and the person speaking never finished expressing her point of view.

We stopped briefly at a rest area to use the bathroom, where my sister-in-law gave us meat and cheese pies and a couple of Honey Buns. The moment we arrived to the Schoolhouse Cottage, which we'd rented, I told everyone I was going for a walk. I wanted to see the little town that Melissa, the house owner, described over the phone. She talked about the little café's and art galleries, the wine tasting tours, the hikes and the nearby beaches. We had driven for five hours, and I was ready to explore. My niece said she would accompany me. We got to the main street, which resembled a picturesque street that belonged to a small European town with no fast food restaurants or chain stores.

One particular corner caught my eyes. The outside had several metal welded art pieces on its walls and the center of its courtyard had a bike, butterfly, and the body of a woman sleeping on her side. I took pictures of the area before I entered a store called Casey-Daniels. It had colorful handmade handbags and matching hats as well as handmade jewelry.

A man in his sixties wearing a beret and glasses greeted us. He was physically well-built and had white hair, white eyebrows, and a white goatee. When I told him we had just arrived for a weekend vacation, he immediately dove into a long conversation about the town of Suttons Bay. His name was Will, and he had been living in this area for fifty years. He made his own jewelry and pointed to a table where he sat all day to do the work. He told us about his neighborhood, the dozens of artists and writers who lived and worked there and the diners that served good food. He brought out a map and asked what we planned to see while we were here, adding, "You and your niece seem to value exploration."

He told us that it would be a great idea to rent bikes from the place across the street and that we shouldn't worry about keeping the bikes outdoors overnight. "No one steals bikes here," he said. He said he would show us where to go and how to get there, *if you choose to*, and he kept telling us to return, *if you wish*, he emphasized.

I asked if I could write about him on my blog, and he said, "You can do whatever you want. You're a writer?"

"Yes."

"What do you write?"

I told him about my books, including the poetry book coming out in about a month. He went to a corner and returned with two magazines. He handed me one and my niece the other. It was called *Exposures, a Leelanau County Student Journal*, and it had been around for twenty-six years. He said he was the publisher. I flipped through it and saw poems written by school students along with pictures, paintings, and other art work.

"There are no ads in here," I said. "How are you able to publish this?"

"It's funded by the schools."

I frowned and closely observed it. "How did you manage that?"

He opened his eye glasses from the center of the frame and removed them. "We submitted a proposal to the school and they accepted."

"Was the journal already in print before you submitted the proposal?"

"No."

I was in awe, totally impressed. I wanted to stay and talk to him some more, but I knew we had to return home. I told him I would stop by the next day. At night, I flipped through the journal and thought about my publishing company. I had always said that the Iraqi-American community needed a voice and watched as, decade after decade, Western authors wrote about Iraqi history, Iraqi people, and Iraqi culture while the Iraqis stood in silence. They were unable to tell their own stories because of language, skill, and cultural barriers. I knew this, and I knew how to write and how to publish. Now that it was so easy to publish, I could take matters into my own hands and publish a series of books about Iraqi Americans. There was definitely a need, and I had the necessary background to make this a success. I could serve this community by giving them a voice through publishing and film. Furthermore, I could grow a successful business.

The next morning I woke up before anyone else. I made myself a cup of coffee and, with the mug in my hand, walked the peaceful streets to Will's store. It was closed and would not open until 10 am, in another two hours. I found a nearby little bench on the sidewalk, next to a stream of water, to sit and read. When the time was right, I returned to the store, but the door was still locked. I peeked through the glass window at the weathervanes, antiques, and unique gifts, such as a medal flying horse. Soon, Will drove up in his bike, and with a big smile greeted me warmly.

"I wanted to talk to you some more about your publishing business," I said.

"Sure," he said, and he suggested we sit on the bench under the sun. The bench was surrounded by a railing of medium sized rocks and a small hill of chip wood. I placed my mug on round cement, the base for one of the metal art pieces that swirled about six feet up.

I told him my story, about writing books for over twenty years and how I'd easily found agents but never the right publisher. When I heard how he found funding for his magazine through the schools, I realized I could also find the right funding for my work if I honed in my audience. I did not have to depend any longer on so-called traditional publishers.

"They say that they want a unique voice, one that has a new perspective, etcetera and my books fit perfectly into that category," I said. "Yet when I submit to them, they say, 'no, that's not quite what we're looking for.' So I realized it's not true. They don't want a unique voice with a new perspective."

"They want an unbiased voice according to their definition of unbiased," he said. "There's an ethnic centric attitude here, and that's what happened when I wanted to introduce the Japanese or Vietnamese jewelry. People said no, that won't work here. Yet most of the jewelry they talked about and liked originated in Japan."

A middle-aged couple approached the store and he paused, looked at them, and said, "You're welcome to go inside and look around. The jewelry is all handmade. I made it myself. If you have any questions, just let me know."

Smiling, they nodded and went inside.

"You can go in and see if they want anything," I said.

He waved his hand. "I'd much rather sit here and talk to you." He told me about traveling with his friend every year to countries like Egypt and Ecuador, regions where their wives were not interested to go. I asked if he went to Egypt before or after the revolution. He said after.

"How was it?" I asked. "Was it dangerous?"

"The illusion of danger is more associated with your own personal behavior," he said, smiling. "Most people don't have antennas when they travel. They don't immense themselves in the experience, and they end up in the wrong place at the wrong time."

The middle-aged couple came out, thanked him, and said goodbye as they strolled into the main street.

"Regarding your work, there's an attitude in this country that the Middle East is so stereotyped that we refuse to acknowledge its historical literature," he said. "We want to group what constitutes the Middle East in simplistic mindset. You have to have an audience who doesn't dismiss it outright, people who are artistic enough to accept alternative viewpoints." He pointed to the building across from us. "This building is green, right? But I tell you it's blue. That's what you're confronting."

He stood up and faced me. "You are a woman of Iraqi descent. We're at an airport and I'm walking toward you, you're walking toward me. There's an elusive glass wall between us. The glass wall is not a wall; it's a mirror. I see me but not you. I only see myself because, for me, it's a one-way mirror. You see me because for you, it's a two-way mirror. You see people from your side of the mirror and my side. You have evolved. You came from a different language. You had thought and philosophical barriers. Guess who mastered both? You. You understood eons by mastering both cultures. People are so consumed with their situation they don't want to hear another viewpoint. It's because of cultural superiority and consumerism."

He told me the story of when he'd dealt with diamonds.

"It's exhausting to deal with people who put their faith in diamonds because of blood diamonds and all that," he said, "but anyway, one day I was selling diamonds to a couple, and the phone rang. I was told that my mother was dead. I told the couple, 'I'm sorry, my mother died. I need to end our meeting.' They said, 'But we promise, it'll only take a minute.' I said, 'I'm sorry, but I need to end our meeting now.' They said, 'Are you sure we can't change your mind?' I opened the door and told them to get out. Their interest trumped my interest. Political interest trumped everything else."

I watched his expressive blue eyes behind the glasses as he continued. "It's not evident to people in Indiana what you're writing. They think, 'Oh my God, the gas went up three cents.' You're confronting a culture that's apathetic because there is an overabundance, not because they don't care. It's like going to the store and finding twenty different types of toothpastes. Why would I need this many types of toothpastes? I need only one kind.

"You're dealing with an audience that has too much of everything. Too much toothpaste, too much everything. I'm an artist. I've been an artist all of my life. I have ten gentle forms of income to allow myself to make an income, like sweat equity. In order to make an income, you have to have a venue, a vehicle. What have you been identifying as a venue? Ninety seven people out of a hundred fail because they don't practice when they should. They go out with friends when they're supposed to practice the piano. They have five kids and the children need attending to."

As I tried to catch up with notetaking, he continued. "People don't care about the integrity of politics. They care about the entertainment of politics. You are so attuned to your multitudes of cultures that you see eons. You talk to an average person and you might as well be talking to a wall. I can feel your views leaking out of you, because how do you talk to the insane? Your job is to find a way around that. That culturally ignorant audience has already made their minds up. Whose ear are you trying to work on? There's one word I want to leave you with – apathy, from their part, not yours."

"So what do I do in this case?"

"It's important to get your foot through the door. Is it relevant which door you get your foot into?"

I considered that.

"I make weird things. I'm not going to stick myself in art shows. You know why? Because I'm not looking for the approval of others. No, I'm going to authenticate me. You're going to authenticate yourself. If I want to put my art at a gallery, then I'm placing what I do at the throne of someone else. They stand and say, 'Oh, that's this and that.' And I lose myself."

I remembered what Janet had told me last year. "When a shaman reaches the mountain top, she doesn't need approval."

"You're the woman walking down the hallway seeing both sides," he said. "Most people are walking and seeing one mirror, not knowing there's a two-way mirror. They figure, my kids are accomplished, they go to private schools, drive Mercedes, go to fancy restaurants. To people who might have everything, how do you get them to spend quality time with children or sit on the bench with them like we're doing right now to have a conversation? That's because they don't value delayed gratification. The more you delay gratification, the better you become.

"Discipline in the face of apathy. You have in your corner discipline. Discipline allows you to go through obstruction – in your case, obstruction of apathy. We are born into time. Whatever we do with our time is our choice. Great Spirit gave you all these things and the intellect, and you look down from the clouds and see it all. That's your burden. I think you know how to make smart choices. We're trapped by originality. Almost everything we get is bits and pieces of other things out there. Our job is to synthesize, put them together in a new way."

The phone rang, startling me. My family wanted to know when I would be returning home. I told Will I had to leave, but that I was grateful for his time and advice and felt that I had come all the way to Suttons Bay just to meet him.

"The truth is, we are obligated to share our gifts," he said. "Otherwise, what on earth is the merit of not sharing it?"

He asked if I could return again, perhaps have dinner with him and his wife. I said I would try. He said, "You will if you want to."

I smiled, knowing what he meant. He had left me with a new perception of my work to ecstatically take home with me.

Chapter 13
SLEEPING BEAR DUNES

After breakfast, we set up for Sleeping Bear Dunes, a park which covers a thirty-five-mile stretch of Lake Michigan's eastern coastline as well as North and South Manitou islands. It was an adventure getting lost, finding the place, and then climbing up and rolling down the sandy mounds that reminded us of Baghdad's deserts. We picked up stones, threw them into the lakes, rolled up our pants, and walked barefoot alongside Lake Michigan. My son placed his Coke can between the rocks and soon it was floating in the middle of the water.

We collected colorful rocks, and I stuffed mine into my pocket. We had so much fun that I thought, if only we could do this once a week, or more realistically, once a month. Get away from the usual routine, relish a new atmosphere and breathtaking nature, enjoy quality family time, and rest and have fun. As we climbed toward our cars, I was deleting old pictures from my iPhone to make room for new footage when I came across a picture of my mother, taken during my daughter's birthday the week prior. In the picture, my mother stared sadly to the ground. I had been too busy with the birthday to notice how miserable she looked, despite the house being full of boisterous children and an amazing reptile show that included a Burmese python named Cinderella.

She hadn't gained all her strength since she returned from the hospital. After last year's therapy, she had learned how to walk, though with assistance because her body was too wobbly and imbalanced for her to carry her own weight. Now she had to once again start from scratch, take baby steps to stand up and move her feet. I knew she was exhausted, and I, too, was exhausted. Some nights I went to bed crying from the pain. On a few occasions, my back ached badly and I worried that I'd hurt it somehow. I began to do more yoga and back exercises. The pain persisted for over a month before it subsided. But it wasn't just the physical pain that bothered me. I had to schedule myself in a way that limited my travels to places as simple as the gym. I was constantly running around to accommodate my children's activities and my mom's meal, bathroom, and bed times. If we had a gathering to attend, or if I had to cover a story that required several hours, I had to make phone calls to have someone be with her when I couldn't. This caused great restrictions on how my family and I could spend our free time. I was fortunate that my husband loved my mother very much and was a strong believer of people taking care of their elders, that it was a God-given requirement, privilege, and blessing, but at times, he did complain. He wondered why my siblings did not help as much as they ought to and raised other questions that only placed a greater burden on me because I did not have the answers.

Tears came down my face as I looked into the bright sun and thought of all the wonderful gifts my mother had given me, lastly the opportunity to serve her. I thanked her for our time together. She said she would be leaving soon, and once she was gone, I would be fine, and she would never forget the love that we'd shared. I kissed the picture, gave her permission to leave this earth whenever she felt it was her time to go, and I continued to follow everyone to the car.

In the car, I went online to research the history of Sleeping Bear Dunes. The park is named after a Chippewa legend of the sleeping bear. According to legend, an enormous forest fire drove a mother bear and her two cubs into the lake for shelter, to reach the opposite shore. After many miles of swimming, the two cubs waded behind and eventually drowned. The mother bear arrived to shore and waited for her cubs to appear.

"That's a touching and nice story," said the Red Indian when I told it to him back at home. "A lot of tourist places have a mythical story, which is the attraction."

"The Great Spirit created two islands," I continued. "North and South Manitou islands to commemorate the cubs, and the winds buried the sleeping bear under the sands of the dunes, where she waits to this day."

"That doesn't sound like a gift from the Great Spirit," he said. "It sounds like a mother that couldn't take care of her cubs."

He said that the Manitou in Canada originally came from the Michigan region, the Manitou Island, which translates as "the Creator's Island." When the English and the Americans were fighting during the Revolution and other wars, most Indians didn't want to join either side so they went to Manitou Island in Ontario just to get away from the fighting.

"It was not a real war, but a war on paper to set a border," he said. "In their mind, you can't have a country unless you have a border so there could be policing and taxing."

Some Indians were friends with the French, some were friends with the Spanish, with the English. During the big war, the Indians fought with each other because they were the only ones there. When the fighting was over, and the Indians wanted to return, the Americans would not allow them to return because they had an alliance with King George at that point. So the natives had to stay in Canada.

"People in the clan system are still here," he said. "They haven't gone anywhere. It's the Sleeping Bear. It's sleeping because you're not using it. There are very powerful things there, but no one is using them. They can say there were little bears frolicking around there, whatever, but the Sleeping Bear is always here. It never left. It's still waiting for good things. And these people that make war, they don't want to wake up the Sleeping Bear, because then the truth will come out."

"What do you mean?"

"The power of the air – radio, TV, advertising – has made people do whatever their next door neighbor does," he said. "It's hard to live in this society and stay really close to the earth."

After the trip to Suttons Bay, I began to surround myself with like-minded people, to stop hiding behind family. Lynn was right about *puellas,* the eternal child characteristic who is afraid to go out into the world, to mingle with adults and shine. A long-time friend and fellow writer, Elisabeth, had months ago moved a block away from my house, on the same street as my children's school. She invited me over for lunch, and I graciously accepted although I kept bumping the visit to the following month or the following week, busy hiding behind family affairs. Finally we set a date, and as I got in my car to drive to her house, although it was so close I could have easily walked, the school called and said that my daughter had a little fever. I picked up my daughter and we went to Elisabeth's house, who welcomed us with open arms and delicious soup.

Elisabeth is a most fascinating woman, a poet and novelist. Born in France, she is of Belgium heritage, and she is married to a doctor from India. She has a special bond to India and travels often, even built a second home there. She used to be the editor-in-chief of the *Gazette van Detroit* and had assigned me freelance work.

Elisabeth, myself, and my daughter had a most lovely lunch over a most lively conversation. Then my daughter laid on the couch as Elisabeth told me about her recent commitment to writing and how that created a synchronicity which brought along several writing proposals and ideas, including starting a mystery novel series based on exotic crimes that occur in India.

"In India when you read the newspaper, you see the strangest crimes," she said.

"Like what?"

"Like these two guys went into a grocery store to rob the owner and threw red peppers in his eyes."

I laughed. "Now I see what you mean about exotic crimes."

Chapter 14
RACEHORSE OR TURTLE

One assignment asked that we find out whether we are a racehorse or a turtle. A turtle type of person understands stillness. They are better suited to the process of aging well. They're what the world calls a "late bloomer." The term refers to young children who developed skills such as language, reading, or social interaction later than others of their age. Thomas Edison and Albert Einstein fell into this category. In adolescence, late bloomer refers to children who suffer from delayed puberty, who are late in reaching their full heights, as was the case with W.B. Yeats and Mark Twain. In adulthood, it's a person who does not discover their talents and abilities until later than normally expected, maybe even during retirement. Julia Childs was in her forties when her passion for cooking began, and Colonel Sanders had a varied resume until he found success, in his sixties, in the fried chicken business.

Racehorses are predatory and have to channel their stress creatively so that it will not hurt or destroy them. What determines a good racehorse is not size. They could be small and bulky or tall and slender, but to have the potential to be a spectacular athlete they must have balance. They need to have a balance and proportion of shape that makes the sum of the parts greater than the whole. Thoroughbred horses are bred to be racing machines, so their hearts are large and heavy, weighing an average of ten pounds. The structure of the heart allows for approximately seventy-five gallons of blood to pump through the horse's body each minute.

No energy is better or worse than the other. It's simply important to recognize your qualities because you can't give them away or stop acting on your qualities, but you have to live a bit differently. Once you know if you are a racehorse or a turtle, and I knew I was a racehorse, you had to do an assignment and answer questions.

How do you create stress?

I created stress by piling up deadlines and to-do tasks, which once included everything from writing to catering to everyone's needs to having my house always be in top-shape condition. Oftentimes, I tried to do all this independently. I've learned to change that stress to be more creative by letting go of the nurturing mother roles that no longer serve me, that were holding me back from fulfilling my dreams, and I redirected that energy toward more Rainbow energies.

How do you change that stress to be more creative?

The decision to completely embrace and honor my Rainbow self rather than adhere to the cultural role of nurturing mother freed me. Of course, I still nurtured my home and family and did so quite meticulously. But I did not step one foot outside of that. Although I'd produced more work than ever before, although at times it felt quite overwhelming, it was the type of work I enjoyed most. The best part was that I didn't feel guilty about saying "no" to tasks that I didn't want to participate in. I didn't care what others thought of me or my work, and I was lenient on myself when I couldn't get something done. I also learned to be flexible and incorporate fun into my daily rituals.

How do you allow the life force to run through you?

Through the shaman breath of power, where one breathes deeply, in through the nose and out through the mouth, holding our intent in our solar plexus, holding the energy coming up from Mother Earth and down from Father Sky, then repeating this ten to twenty times. By sending and receiving love from nature and through prayer, meditation and gratitude. By doing yoga, swimming, or walking.

How do you whip up that energy?

By clearing, organizing, and cleaning the house, cooking a delicious meal, eating healthy food, stepping outside for a few fresh breaths.

How do you save and hold your power?

Through prayer and patience. I also stayed away from anything that was not my business and focused on the task at hand. As a racehorse, I could easily fall into the trap of doing too much and driving myself crazy in the process. So I began to study about and incorporate turtle tendencies into my life. I appreciated the movement of the turtle and gravitated toward her lifestyle more and more each day. Maybe soon I would be a happy turtle.

I wanted to be a turtle because I had pushed my writing abilities to an extreme. I'd revised my first two novels and re-published them, published a third novel, gathered my published poetry and placed them in one poetry book, and collected the material for my Iraqi-Americans book series, which required that I interview many, many people. I began to build my platform and online presence and even brought the documentary *The Great American Family* from out of the gutters.

I wanted to be a turtle, to do what Leslie had recently advised. She said, "After graduating, honor what you have accomplished. Breathe. Be. Sit in ceremony with the Sisterhood. They will help you to see what will be your next body of work."

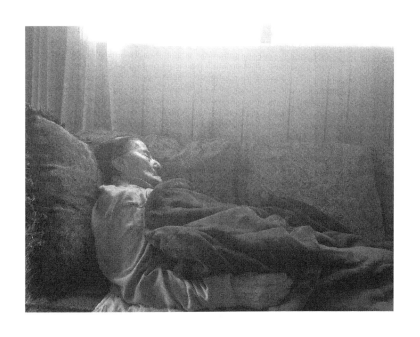

Chapter 15
READY TO DIE

At 2:04 am, I was once again up in the middle of the night, listening to my eighty-two year old mother's loud gurgling sound, otherwise known as the death rattle, from the adjacent room. Tears ran down my face as I wondered, will today be her last day on earth? I got a few hours of sleep before it was time to wake up and get my children ready for school.

My son, a kindergartner, cried, "I don't want to go to school! It's bowing!"

My daughter, a third grader, wanted to wear a fancy dress with ruffles. I explained that *this* dress was not appropriate for school. She threw a tantrum, my son continued with his "School is bowing!" mantra, and then my husband appeared.

"I'm going to be late for work," he said. "If they're not ready in five minutes, I'm leaving without them and you'll have to drop them off at school."

I tossed out all my niceties and started hollering demands until the kids were dressed, their lunches packed, and everyone was out of the house. Once I closed the door, I inhaled the silence as though it was oxygen I had not had for days. I made myself a cup of coffee and sat at my computer to write. The phone rang. It was Doctor Bakker, the tall and skinny podiatrist with white hair who reminded me of a mad scientist, not only because of his appearance but because of his high intellect. He was a member of Mensa, the high IQ society. He had been working on my mother's bedsore, on her left foot, which had developed during her stay at the hospital.

"How's your mother doing?" he asked.

"She was in the emergency room a few days ago."

"She was?"

"The visiting doctor thought she had pneumonia, so she sent her to the ER. The ambulance picked her up and, later that same day, the ER doctor released her. He said all the tests came back negative."

"Hmmm, that's peculiar."

"I was initially happy to hear him say that, but now I'm worried again. Her rattling hasn't gone away, and she's behaving strangely. Yesterday she did not want to lie down, and she asked me to take her outside. Usually she's tired and prefers staying inside."

I had read that people, when they are nearing death, have a sudden burst of energy.

"Do you think I can see her in about half an hour or so?" he asked.

"Yes. She's still sleeping, but it's noon so I should get her up."

She was so weak that I wasn't sure if I would be able to safely get her into the wheelchair. Normally she helped a little. That part went okay and, after the usual grooming routine, I brought her to the kitchen table and placed the usual breakfast in front of her, sliced Spanish cheese and tomatoes, pita bread and a cup of tea and milk. She did not say the normal "God bless you and your children" when I helped her up or served her food. She was exceptionally silent.

I cleared some dirty dishes, picked up the Lego pieces and

school papers off the floor, and made myself another cup of coffee. When I glanced in her direction, I noticed she couldn't lift the Spanish cheese slice to her mouth. It was hanging by her fingers in midair. Her expressionless face and droopy mouth worried me.

"Mom, what's wrong?" I asked.

"I'm tired," she said, her voice exhausted.

I removed the breakfast for fear she would choke on it. By the time I was done, she was fast asleep. There was a knock on the door, and I quickly opened it, knowing it was Doctor Bakker. I welcomed him inside and prepared the items that he normally needed, like disposable bed pads to place under her foot and a Styrofoam cup with half-an-inch of water. As he dug out the dead skin with his scalpel, my mother continued to sleep. Dr. Bakker said, "She must be really tired from the last two day's excitement."

An hour passed and she was still asleep. After he left, I tried to wake her up but to no avail. She did not respond. In times like this, I wondered, is this her time to go? Should I honor that this is the case or try to revive her? Since she'd moved into my home, she had, on several occasions, told me that she wanted to die. Twice or three times, she called me to sit in front of her because, she said, "I'm going to die."

I obliged, sat in front of her, and cried my eyes out for hours as I awaited her death. Yet she remained alive for days, weeks, and months. Evidently there was a miscommunication between her and the spirit world, a realm she visited often. I know this because, every now and then, when she opened her eyes from a long and deep sleep, I saw tears. One time I asked her who had she seen in her dream and she said sadly, but with exquisite memory, "Your father and my tribe."

I asked if she would like to leave this earth and go to the other world. She said, "Yes, why not? Whatever God prefers."

I moved her to her bed and at 3:15 pm, I picked up the kids from school. When they entered the house and didn't see her lying on the couch, where she normally was, they asked, "Where's nanna?"

"She's tired. She's in her bed."

I checked on my mother, and she looked comatose. I didn't know what to do, whether to call the family. A knock on the door startled me.

"Who is it?" I asked.

"It's Stella."

Relieved to hear the nurse's voice, I quickly opened the door. "It's so good to see you!"

"I know I didn't call," she said. "I was in the area, and I knew you get home at this time after you pick up the kids from school. So I thought I'd check in on your mom since she just got out of the hospital. How is she doing?"

"Not too good."

"What's wrong?"

I led her to the bedroom, and she took my mother's vitals and looked into her eyes. Stella was a Native American with long hair, long nails, and a long nursing career. She'd cared for her mother for thirty years. She said, reluctantly, "It doesn't look too good. It's a matter of a few days, maybe less…"

I broke down crying, and my daughter appeared out of nowhere and hugged me.

"What's wrong, Mommy?" she asked.

"Nanna might not stay with us for long."

"No, Mom! No! I want her to stay!"

She burst into tears, deeper than I expected from her.

"Don't be sad," I said to her. "That's what Nanna wants. She wants to go and be in peace with God and to see my Babba, her husband, and the rest of her family."

"Don't you have a sister there too?" she asked.

I paused, and then I remembered my deceased sister. "Yes, I do. They've all been waiting for her a long time, and now it's their turn to spend time with her."

My daughter cried even harder. I hugged and kissed her.

"We're lucky we had this time with her," I said. "She gave me many gifts, and living with us was one of her biggest gifts."

The nurse said that I'd better tell the family so we could decide what we should do, whether to take her to the hospital or leave her at home. Her phone rang, and she answered the call. I stepped out to go to the bathroom and, on the way there, I saw smoke in the kitchen. I hurried to the stove and turned it off. Our lunch of chicken and potatoes was now burned, and the smoke lingered heavily throughout the house. I opened the doors and windows to let in fresh air.

When Stella left, I called my sisters. They came one by one, sad and distraught. One broke into such loud sobbing, you'd think she was at a funeral. I asked her to please stop. "You're scaring Mom!"

My brothers then started coming over, then my nieces and nephews. One of my nieces and my nephew encouraged us to take my mother to the hospital. I explained that she was just there and they found nothing wrong with her. My fear was that she would die there. We argued about whether the wisest choice was to handle this in a medical fashion or allow nature to take its course. In the end, I called her visiting doctor and told her the situation.

"I can't believe the ER sent her back without giving her

anything," she said. "I'm going to prescribe an antibiotic. Give her two today and then one every day until it's done."

She called in the prescription, and I made it to the pharmacy minutes before they closed. I gave my mother the medicine, everyone went home, and I called one of the apprentices who volunteered for hospices, wanting to learn more about this service in case we needed it.

The next day, Saturday, was again hectic. Family arrived early in the morning, and I had to interview someone for my book in the afternoon. I eagerly left the house at the appointed interview time, unable to handle the situation – my mother in her death bed and the number of people going in and out of my home.

When I returned from the interview, I saw everyone laughing and joking.

"She's doing real good," one sister said. "She ate biscuits and drank milk. I fed her the soup I brought from home. She's up and looking at us, smiling, and she even said a few words."

I almost passed out from relief and anxiety. Over the course of two years, my mother had a number of near-death experiences which had completely drained me. I could not handle another episode, and I wondered how many more were in store for me.

The nurse came over the next day. When I told her what had happened, she observed my mother with a smile and said, "The other day when I left your house and went home, I told my husband that that poor woman would last only a few hours, that her family might not even make it in time to see her. All her vitals indicated that. For her to make such a turnaround within a matter of days is nothing short of a miracle. I've been a nurse for over forty years, and I've never seen someone make such a turnaround. I don't know that any antibiotic can do that.

Something else made that happen."

She was right. Having her children all around her, praying for her and asking her to stay…maybe my mother had changed her mind. She did not want to go.

That weekend depleted me and forced me to make changes. I decided that no matter what happened from now on, I would not think about my mother's death or be too fazed about her health conditions. I also decided to take better care of myself. I took my mother in because I wanted her to die with dignity, not so I would turn into a workhorse. I began to take long walks, do yoga more regularly, and asked for help without the fear of inconveniencing anyone. I set boundaries. I told my siblings that having too many visitors put a strain on me, and that if they wished to visit our mother they would have to do so in alternate ways, like perhaps take her to their home for a few hours. They all live within a few miles from me, and even though it was difficult to get her in and out of the car and the SMART Bus was almost always booked, the effort was worth it for everyone involved, especially her.

They nodded their heads, agreed with me, acted as if they had full sympathy and compassion, then tossed my requests out the window as if they were cigarette ashes. In our culture, it is believed that taking care of a parent is an honor and blessing. Despite the challenges, my mother's presence had deeply enriched our lives. My siblings, on the other hand, might end up traumatizing me for life. I loved them dearly, even adored them at times. They had a long list of great qualities, including big hearts, cleverness, and intuitiveness, but they could also be awfully stubborn. They refused to understand how their popping up at my door at inconvenient times was an inconvenience.

The act of hospitality is especially sacred in our culture, with roots dating back to ancient biblical times. Prophet Abraham met his guests in lavish ways that seem exaggerated to most Westerners. He not only welcomed them with enthusiasm, but bowed down to the ground, and of course, offered the typical generosity of Oriental hospitality, food, water, and shelter. One was not to show the slightest ill manner toward guests, whether they were family, relatives, friends, or strangers. So I had to try to be kind and pleasant when I felt the opposite of that.

Still, while at times it was strenuous, other times it was educational and entertaining. My siblings had unique stories and tidbits to share. Once my oldest brother told me how a new immigrant to America said to him, "What kind of country is this that they sell their children?"

"No, they don't sell children in this country," my brother said.

"Yes, they do!" the man said.

"They do!" the man's wife restated. "We saw it the other day in a television commercial that said Sears Kids Sale."

Chapter 16
LETTER OF INTENT

I dreamt that my mother died. I told my family as I sobbed, knowing this time it was for real. As the funeral preparations were underway, I was incredibly sad. I woke up from the dream with tears in my eyes, the same tears I had when a few years ago I dreamt she was in my arms, like a baby. I got out of bed, went into her room, and listened to her breathe.

I pulled myself away and went to my computer. I had no deadlines, and for the first time in a long time, I felt relaxed and free. The birds greeted me with their chirps, and the wooden chimes clicked musically in my ears. The black squirrel searched for food underneath the patio table, and the tree branches swayed like a woman's embroidered hand fan.

A canary landed on one of the chairs and faced east. Its yellow color brightened my mood even more so. It flew to the tree, stood still a while, and then flew away in the east direction. I looked up his totem and found that a canary totem represents the power of your song and voice. When the canary shows up as your totem, she wants you to continue speaking from the heart and shed sour notes within you and continue to spread joy with your words. Doing this will also enhance and awaken your intuition. Fresh air is very important to canary people.

That day, I made it to the gym after two weeks of not

working out. Despite the decisions I had made, I still struggled to get fresh air and a good workout. This left a residue of fatigue on my body. I could only do a 3.5 speed on the treadmill and, during yoga, I had to step out of the class for a few moments to drink water. I had never done that before. My body had not recuperated from the enormous amount of pressure it had endured the last two weeks with deadlines and children, not to mention my mother's dying episodes, although the subsequent ones were not as dramatic.

As if my list of to-dos was not long enough, I had volunteered to help my daughter's cheerleading coach only to find out there was no coach to help. I'd be the one coaching the cheerleaders, although I had never been a cheerleader, nowhere near it. I accepted the position because the sports programmer said they were short of coaches and I wanted to show my daughter how to not be afraid to lead and try something new. I stayed in the game despite the drama created by the mother of the one cheerleader who was worried that, without prior experience, I did not have the necessary skills to make my team wow the audiences at cheer-off. She was polite and sweet and did not say this outright to my face, but I could tell by her reaction, when I asked her what a cheer-off was, that she was greatly perturbed. She immediately contacted the programmer, confronted her with a list of the issues at stake, and was basically booted off the team.

I went on YouTube to learn the moves and the chants and to see what a cheer-off was. My attempt encouraged my sister-in-law and other women I knew to sign their daughters up, and we met at Dahlia Park twice a week for practice. When it neared cheer-off, I gathered the girls at my house too, where we practiced in the backyard. We had lots of fun.

During cheer-off later in the year, in autumn, our team was the last to take the stage. This gave us an opportunity to witness cheerleading teams that did terrific performances but also ones that did awful performances, which gave us more confidence in our routine. My brother, nephew, husband, and son had sat on the bleachers and they, too, were relieved by the few awful performances, knowing that I could not possibly do as bad as that.

* * *

One Sunday in July, we went to Spencer Park, arriving just as the sun had begun to fade. Without the scorching heat, I enjoyed a walk with my son around the one-mile bike path. The abundant tree leaves rustled, and the seagulls flew over our heads. I listened to the wind and remembered the many times I had walked with my sisters down this path. I missed them. When I was the age of my daughter and my younger brother the age of my son, my older siblings, my sisters in particular, would take us to Stoney Creek beach. My younger brother and I had a blast building sand castles and swimming in the beach.

My father's energy then appeared, telling me how proud he was of me. I stopped and faced his direction so I could give him my full attention. He said, "You did it. You succeeded all by yourself. You wrote five books, which is more than I could have dreamed for you."

I listened, feeling every word and his love. I realized that what I had done was great, and I could retire tomorrow and the value of that greatness would remain. Anything else was icing on the cake.

"Mamma, do you like chicken?" my son asked.

"Yes."

"When we go to California, they serve chicken and you can dip it in ranch sauce. Mamma, do you like jalapenos?"

"Yes, I do."

"They serve chicken with jalapenos."

"Where's this at?"

"Skylanders," he said vigorously. "Do you like coffee?"

I smiled, realizing this was an enticement to get me to agree to something. "Yes."

"They have coffee for free. What kind of cup do you like to drink it in?"

"A mug."

"They have that."

"Do they?"

"Yes, do you like buffet?"

"Yes."

"They have that too, one for adults and one for children."

We were quiet as we continued our walk.

"Can we go there, Mamma?" he asked.

"We'll talk to Babba about it."

I didn't write in my journal for the remainder of the summer. I couldn't. The interviews with people, the manuscripts produced, notes about my books, etc. had overloaded me with too many words. Then there were the assignments that had to do with storytelling and *words*. As instructed, I would write, over and over again, a favorite word in different shapes, sizes, and languages like English, Arabic, and Aramaic. I'd say them out loud, and then I'd write them in a poem. I did this until I decided I could no longer do this exercise.

This year had really pushed me to my edge, made me desperately look forward to Storm Eagle, which was right around the corner. Lynn asked us to write a letter of intent for her to read. What did we want to accomplish within a year or five after graduation? The first thing I wanted to do was rest and rest well. This didn't mean that I'd stop working; I loved to work. It meant I'd have more fun, splurge on myself, not feel bogged down by so many responsibilities, to just *be* for a while. Once my body, mind, and spirit replenished with a good rest and lots of fun, I would spend the next five years revisiting more projects that sat in my drawers in need of execution. I would allow things to happen smoothly and naturally, to simply trust in the process.

During Lynn's last conference call before the Storm Eagle gathering, someone asked why *puellas* unbalanced themselves with self-importance. What is the solution to heal themselves? Lynn said it was because of self-pity. "Self-importance is the ego covering up a situation or an action that comes from a feeling of lack, of not being good enough," she said. "Why does that happen with *puellas*? Because you've been told that you're entire life. As a child, you had to be careful to keep from being hit or hurt in some way. Self-importance destroys your power and your life."

"What's the difference between self-importance and confidence?" I asked Lynn.

"With self-importance, because you don't feel good enough, you behave as if you're better than everybody else. It's thinking that maybe you are better than everybody else and you think, why is everybody treating me so badly when I'm so perfect? I do the best job of anybody, and I don't know why they're not treating me any better. Does that make sense?"

"Yes, thank you."

"The other word you mentioned, confidence – if you have true confidence, then you're humble. You feel the need and desire to elevate other people around you to help them become better. The self-important person wants to diminish you so they can stand above you. Confidence is feeling at ease and comfortable with yourself. You're not trying to outshine anybody, you're just shining. If nobody notices, that's fine and if somebody does, that's great too. There's nothing more irresistible in life than being confident."

She later said that, "To be a shaman, to be a healer, a magical person in life, you have to heal yourself first. It's like being on an airplane and how you put the oxygen provided in the ceiling on yourself first and then on your child."

She also said that a lot of people don't understand the noble quality of the soul. "This life is an extraordinary gift," she said. "Yet some people are trying to ruin that because they don't understand that it's a gift to be alive. You don't come waltzing back into the dimension of relativity."

Before the call was up, I told Lynn that whenever I saw her picture pop up online or heard her voice or received an email from her, questions bubble up inside of me and I have the urge to reach out and talk to her. But I did not know what I wanted to talk to her about, so I put it aside.

"That's why I'm here," she said, "to help you discover what is hidden oftentimes."

I had no idea what that meant, what was in store for me, until I arrived to Storm Eagle.

Chapter 17
STORM EAGLE

My flight prepared for takeoff at around 11:30 am. I thought about last night's dream. Dishes were stacked in a layered area with water coming down from the sides like a waterfall, resembling the Dunn's River Falls in Jamaica, where my sisters and I and other tourists held hands and climbed to the top. My daughter and I stood there with a few other women. My daughter made a minor mistake, and I grew angry. I saw from her watery eyes and expression that she was hurt. I had hurt her, even embarrassed her, over the proper way of washing dishes.

I woke up from that dream feeling distraught. I had stayed up late the night before feeling guilty about snapping at my son for spilling his Dr. Pepper which we'd gotten for lunch from McDonald's with his kids' meal. My daughter had complained that he'd gotten a large size drink while hers was small. Sometimes McDonald's filled drinks in a large cup when they were out of the smaller ones.

As I mopped the Dr. Pepper off of the floor and part of the chair, I cussed up a storm. Earlier during breakfast, my mother had spilled her cup of tea and milk, and I had to mop that as well. I hated how I'd behaved, especially knowing that I'd be leaving for four days the next morning, but I couldn't help it. The beautiful things I planned in my head during daytime, when my mind was fresh and my body ultra-energetic, often vanished by late afternoon, absorbed by a whirlwind of doing.

The dream bothered me. I got out of bed and went into my daughter's room. Then I laid beside her, kissed her, and hugged her tight. I did not want to do so many things a day and be tired when my children came home from school. Although I agreed to coach her cheerleading team primarily for her sake, and although I took care of her needs and wants as best as I could, sometimes when she came to snuggle with me in the kitchen, while I responded with a quick hug and kiss, my body was so tired that these acts of love felt like work. Sometimes I wanted to cuddle in bed and sleep for hours without anyone calling for me.

I took a deep, grateful breath as the plane landed, knowing that I needn't be so hard on myself. I've done what I set out to do. I've taken the necessary steps and have made room inside of me for the experiences I wish to experience. This phase of my life will pass, and the pressure of doing too much will be alleviated. What will remain are the sacred memories.

Arizona was hot. The driver who picked me up from the airport used to live in Florida and came to this "dry heat" three years ago. As soon as I got into his car, he offered me a bottle of water and gum. We chitchatted a while and, when he found out that I am a writer, he said, "I know this very successful and smart doctor who one day decided to leave his million dollar practice and write. I was very surprised."

"He must have thought this in his head for a long time before he made the leap," I said. "That's wonderful of him, to have pursued his dreams in a practical manner."

"He still owns half of his share."

"That's very smart. When people jump into their dreams without preparation, oftentimes they are surprised about the reality."

"I advised him to do that. He's like my daughter – you can't tell him what to do. But when he said he was leaving his practice, I told him he better keep half his share. He didn't say much that day, but he came to me a few days later and said, 'Todd, of all of my friends, you're the only one who gave me this advice. I'm going to take it.' He's a bright man, a lot younger than me, in his early thirties. Very bright for his age. He asks questions that show he's beyond his years. Like he said to me, 'If you had to do something over again, what would it be?' I said, 'I would have more kids. I have one daughter who's twenty and back when I had her, I hadn't even planned to have any kids. After I had her, I thought no way would I have more. I regret that now because, although it's a lot of work, it's very much worth it. My daughter has been such a blessing in my life."

I arrived to the Franciscan Renewal Center at 4:30 pm.

"Dinner is served at six o'clock," the receptionist said to me as she handed me the key. "There's a room with coffee and tea and vending machines for drinks."

"There's no food?" I asked.

"If you want, there are fruits in the cafeteria."

I was starving, since I'd skipped breakfast, as I normally did, and had had only a vanilla mocha at the airport. I placed my bags in the room and took a stroll. The Franciscan Renewal Center was a tranquil and relaxing place, full of greenery and religious artwork. Formerly a dude ranch, the Franciscan friars bought the twenty-five-acre site in 1951 and, in less than a year began a retreat ministry to the public. The establishment is led by Catholic priests that belong to the brotherhood of the Order of Friars.

Two of the apprentices, upon seeing me, waved from the other side of the courtyard. They invited me into their room and offered me grapes and nuts.

We later went into the conference room, where other women were working, and set up the sacred space using colorful tulle, lights, and other fabrics. I saw Nancy. She was tall and elegant, with shoulder-length hair and a pleasant smile. She was in jeans, which made her look quite youthful. She reminded me of someone, but I couldn't figure out who. Soon I learned that Leslie was not coming to Storm Eagle because her mother had recently passed away. This took me by surprise. I had really hoped to see her there, and her absence felt strange.

After dinner, Lynn gave a short lecture. She told us to leave behind our stories from our trips. "This is one of the most creative times in our history because of our reentry of ancient knowledge into this century," she said. "Science is tapping into that rhythm and flow. The Sisterhood of the Shields don't talk in scientific terms."

She brought up the wars in the Middle East and said, "We are all responsible for the wars in the Middle East because there's a war in each and every one of us that we have not addressed. I am responsible, and together we can work together for the good of all. We are all the tree of dreams."

She talked to us about the Dreamer God, science, the stars, how the Sisterhood of the Shields said that we are made of stars and to the stars we shall return. "And now scientists are discovering that star particles are on our earth," she said.

She also advised that when we look at someone, to look at their potential. Locate their pain, pour our intent into their constellation, and initiate their becoming. She had us sign a sacred contract that stated we would, for the next four days, have an attitude of gratitude. We had to go up to the front of the room, place a talking stick in a mound of mud to plant a new seed, and drop the sacred contract in the basket. Lynn then blessed each of us using her gorgeous feathers.

We went outside, where the fourth-year apprentices were assigned the task of smudging everyone under the night sky. Smudging is a Native American practice where certain herbs are burned to create a cleansing smoke bath. The smoke is used during ceremonies and rituals to purify people, rooms, and even objects by clearing negative energy from the space.

We were surrounded by candles, lovely trees, and grass. Each person stood in a different direction to form a wheel. I was designated the south. A bundle of white sage was placed in earthenware and lit for a few seconds before we extinguished the flame and let the smoke swirl up. Whenever the smoke died, we lit it again to form a healthy buildup of smoke.

We purified ourselves first, going in the center, then around the four directions. Then the others showed up – mentors, teachers' assistants, and apprentices. When they came to the south, they sat on a chair in front of me and waved smoke toward their body. It was a moving experience to stand there and watch each woman approach the chair and sit down with her pretty flat shoes, gym shoes, or sandals. Some had on shawls which flared as they reached down to the sage and guided the smoke toward them. I was honored when Janet took a seat in front of me. Tears rushed down my face as I watched this woman with white hair who had helped me tremendously.

The stillness of the night increased, making the sound of water trickling down from the nearby fountain intensify. When we were done, the mentors said we could leave the sage and candles and they would put it away. We were about to leave when one of the mentors said, "No! No! Wait! Lynn wants to smudge."

I returned to my spot and soon Lynn was beside me smudging herself, the colorful flare sleeve top moving gracefully and delicately as she raised her arms to the sky in a meditative state. I watched her closely, intrigued by her beauty and our mysterious history. Her amused lips shined with glitter makeup as did her eyelids. Her closed eyes smiled as they connected to the world we would only find in dreams. I remembered our first call and the book that had touched my heart and rekindled my love for writing. What brought us here together? Have I met her in a previous lifetime? Who is this woman who has helped transform my life through her books and her school?

Lynn opened her bright blue eyes, which still smiled with knowingness, thanked me, and moved on to the next direction.

Chapter 18
LABYRINTH

Dressed in a three-quarter length white and black summer dress, I stepped outside of Piper Hall building to return my niece's phone call before Lynn showed up for the morning lecture. Lynn walked toward the building and said, "You look so pretty standing like that under the sun."

"You always look pretty," I said.

She laughed. "You're so cute."

But it was true. She was in better physical shape than most of the women half her age, and she had a glamorous way about her that proved one could be from Beverly Hill or Baghdad or wherever and still be connected.

I went inside, the lecture began, and later on, at some point, Nancy called my name and asked that I step outside of the building. In the hallway, she said, "Each year, Lynn chooses an apprentice to work with for the healing circle. It's usually a fourth-year apprentice, but sometimes the apprentice could be from another year. Before she chooses the person, we go around and ask potential candidates if they agree to participate. She doesn't want to pick someone who would say no. If she chose you, would you be willing to participate?"

I frowned, confused and afraid, yet I knew this would be a great opportunity. She looked at me patiently, and I wanted so badly to figure out who she resembled. Something about her brought memories of someone dear to my heart.

"You don't have to say yes, but this is a privilege," she said.

I knew it would be, but Lynn, as beautiful as I thought her to be, scared the daylights out of me. She pushed the buttons that brought deep seated wounds to the surface that I did not want to look at. Sometimes it felt as if these wounds were actually demons, unwilling to let me go and be free. Or were they deities that wanted me to receive the full message so that I could continue to move my work forward?

"Although this is frightening, it would be foolish to say no to this opportunity," I said.

"And she may pick someone else. She just wants to know if you'd accept."

"I accept."

Later in the day, we did the pipe ceremony with Lynn. I was the only one without a pipe, so Nancy offered that I use hers. At home, I had used *narguila*, a hookah, to do my pipe ceremonies. We did not actually light the pipes because we were indoors, but we agreed to gather after lunch by the mountains and light them for our own little ceremony.

During lunch, I sat outside under the sun at one of the white tables by the pool. I wanted to enjoy the beautiful landscape before I left this place. When I finished my chicken salad, I returned inside the cafeteria to grab a bowl of split pea soup and noticed my classmates sitting at a table with Lynn. I decided to join them.

Lynn was talking about her trips, the Alaskan cruise and the pilgrimage to Peru. I told her about a documentary I'd watched where people in the United States went to Peru to take a herb, *ayahuasca*, that opened a gateway to their dark side.

"I don't recommend it," she said, shaking her head and expressing further disapproval of it with her eyes. She had tried it once.

Two of the apprentices at the table said that they had tried it. They said it was very strong and caused them to vomit. One said she had done it five times but never received anything from it.

"Then why did you keep doing it?" Lynn asked.

"I was lost, and I wanted to find my way."

The other apprentice said that while she discouraged anyone from using it, it had helped her. Once it made her look at her fear of death.

I asked Lynn, "If it has this type of effect, why do shamans use it?"

"Because it's their way," she said. "The people of that region, it's part of their lives."

"I sensed from the documentary that people in the West use it as a quick spiritual fix," I said.

"Yes," one of the apprentices who had tried it said. "They want to work on all their issues and become self-realized overnight."

I asked Lynn, "Why do you think that some Native Americans get so upset when non-natives try to pass on their teachings?"

"Because of godly ignorance!" She told me the story of a famous man named Russell who was an activist for Native Americans. He'd said to her, "We've worked so hard all these years to pass on our teachings and yet these people come along and persecute the people who try to do just that."

The fourth-year group and I walked with our mentors to a desert area and set our pipe bags on a sitting bench with a table. We unwrapped the items in the bags, like tobacco, sweet grass, a lighter, and began the ceremony. Afterward, we went to the labyrinth nearby. One of the apprentices brought her flute, others brought their rattles. The woman with the flute led the group. She played charmingly, reminding me of when Chip played his flute.

I had nothing to hold and was last in line. The moment my feet touched the sand, I felt myself walking as a child in the streets of Baghdad, on the way to school, dressed in a uniform, silk ribbons tied around my braids and ponytails. The memory caught me off guard. How did I get here? I thought I had come to terms with that part of my life. I wanted to close that chapter of my life, but it seemed like I never would.

Then I saw my husband as a child and he looked exactly like my son. He was six-years-old, my son's age now. I thought of my daughter, who was the same age now that I was when we left Iraq. I tried to remember when I had first seen my husband in Iraq. Had we ever met? We must have, as we were from the same tribe, but how and when? How old were we? Yesterday at the cafeteria table we were talking about husbands, and I said that I'd been married to my husband for a thousand years.

The flute and rattle sounds kept bringing everything to the surface, the wide boulevards, the grassy traffic circles, but mostly, the vast desert oasis with unpaved roads, some of which I had heard have the biggest and best types of hawks and an abundance of rare birds. By the time we left the labyrinth, I fell into utter silence. I couldn't speak. When we returned to Room H, one of the mentors passed around the talking stick so we would have a chance to express our feelings about the pipe ceremony and the walk around the labyrinth. I glanced at the talking stick but did not touch it. With a glance toward Nancy, whose eyes seemed to comprehend what I had just gone through, I allowed the talking stick to go to the next person.

Nancy reminded me of Chip's companion, Susan, I realized.

Chapter 19
DREAM OF A GURU

The night of the third-year marriage ceremony, after everyone hugged and kissed, Lynn came to me as we were going to the exit door. She looked me up and down and gave me a hug that, to me, was like the hug of death foreshadowing what was to come. She knew. I knew that she knew.

That night I had a strange dream. I was irritated and in a hurry to leave what seemed to be my cousin's house in a busy district in Iraq, perhaps in Harthiya, her parent's home, the area where we, too, lived. I was not irritated by anyone or a particular thing, but I felt the need to leave.

We finally got into the car, but one of my husband's nephews drifted away with the car and left us behind in this strange bazaar. I panicked and looked for my children. Every time I called their names, they appeared from somewhere. They were having fun, playing. I knew they were safe but in this place, I was running to find how to get home. My phone did not work, and neither did my sister's. I saw a relative and asked to use her phone. She gave it to me with annoyance but did not show me how to use it.

A young, wise man offered free classes. I passed him up and then arrived in front of a very important Indian guru who I knew was my guru. I sat in front of him. He was supposed to test me, and all he said was, "Are you ready for tonight?"

I remembered that I had agreed to do the healing circle. I winced in remembrance, the guru's grin widened, I said "yes," and he nodded. I got up and thought, part of me wants this, part of me is terrified. I continued rushing through this place, trying to get out, watching my bare feet go through what seemed like a torn down street with a ceiling.

I woke up late. My roommate walked into the room, crying. She'd had an argument with her partner over the phone. I consoled her briefly but then had to leave. I was late to my breakfast appointment with Nancy. She'd set up private meal times with each of her apprentices. On the way to the cafeteria, I ran into another couple with a dilemma. They were a gay couple who always traveled together. Except for during meal times, the apprentice's companion couldn't participate in any of the classes or other school activities so he had to find ways to busy himself for the four-day gatherings.

"You looked like a great Native American warrior yesterday," I told the apprentice who'd had his marriage ceremony the night before.

"When I came into the room, he freaked out," he said about his partner.

The partner suddenly popped out of the room and asked, "Is it true that I'm not supposed to talk to you guys because you're in sacred space?"

I didn't know what he meant by that, turned it into a joke, and said I had to head to the cafeteria. He said, "I'll come with you."

He followed me, but his partner asked him to come back. He went for a moment, they exchanged some words, and then he caught up with me. "Is it true?" he asked.

I said I didn't know anything about that, and he expressed his woes. In the cafeteria, Nancy sat with a group of mentors. I apologized for being late and said it was okay to reschedule our meeting if she preferred.

"No, no," she said and moved to an empty table, where I joined her.

"I'm so sorry I'm late," I said. "I'd planned to wake up early, like I did yesterday, go out and write, and meet you for breakfast. But I woke up late, and several couples had problems with their partners. I figured it was the energy of last night's marriage ceremony."

"That's okay," she said. "I haven't been here long. I wanted to tell you that you're in the healing circle."

I opened my eyes wide.

"Lynn picked you for the healing circle."

I was quiet for a moment and then I told her about the dream, where the guru said, "Are you ready for tonight?"

"When the guru said that, I winced and afterward I got up and went running barefoot to find a way out of the building, to escape tonight."

"Well, you're not getting out," she said, laughing.

"Ever since you asked if I would accept to be in the healing circle, things began to happen, like at the labyrinth. Even though I did not know that Lynn would work on me, I felt like the proposal had opened a gateway."

"Well, you're definitely very intuitive," she said. "I have to tell you that this is a great honor and a wonderful opportunity. The year I graduated, they asked me to be in the healing circle and they also asked Leslie. She said no way in hell am I getting up there. People were surprised that I said yes because I am a reserved person. When I went up there, we talked about my childhood with my father, and I have to tell you I was so glad I did that."

"I know that working with Lynn and the Sisterhood is a great opportunity, but I'm concerned about all the people who will be watching."

"Everyone there will be holding space for you. You will feel safe. Now, you can't tell anyone about this, and you have to pick an attendant who will escort you to the room afterward. When I did the healing circle, Leslie was my roommate and since she was already in my room and I had a good relationship with her, I picked her. But you can pick anyone you want."

"I'm thinking of the apprentice from Spain because in second year we did a meditation together where she saw my connection to India," I said. "In last night's dream, I sat in front of a guru from India, and the other day when observing Lynn smudge, I asked who this woman was? Is she the guru that I wanted when, twenty years ago, I had read Irina Tweedie's memoir *Daughter of Fire*? Could she have been my guru in a past life?"

"The person you choose for tonight will only hold space for you. They may not even speak a word."

The other reason I brought up the woman from Spain was because we had not spent much time together. She'd been busy going back and forth to the different school year groups to catch up with the work. She had come from far away, and I didn't know when the next time I would see her was.

"I haven't really had the chance to connect with her in person," I said.

"You're looking for a shamanic exchange with her," Nancy said.

"Which is not what this is about."

"No, it's not."

"Then my roommate is the perfect person to be my attendant because the first day we were here, I was able to open up to her about certain issues, like having to take care of my mom and the enormous work I had to deal with, and she handled it great."

"She's a very warm person."

"And she's a lot of fun. Last night we were joking and laughing so much, it reminded me of my teen years and my early twenties, hanging out with friends, taking life lightly."

"When you approach her, you must swear her to secrecy. No one can know about who's in the healing circle. We must not even speak to the mentors about it. In the meantime, you can approach me for any questions."

"I'd rather not think of this at all until the time comes."

People started to go to Piper Hall, and I suddenly felt the fear. It was still early so I decided to sit on a bench that was under the sun and surrounded by citrus trees and get up to date in my journal. Leslie called me and said, "You're going to be in the healing circle."

"Yes."

I felt nervous. I would be running into Lynn throughout the day, and we both knew that we would be working on me in front of the whole school.

I arrived to Piper Hall late and missed the chakra tuning. Lynn came in and gave her usual prayers, meditations, lectures. Then we went to a room to be tested by her. When I entered that room, the only empty chair available around the table was the one next to Lynn's chair. She wasn't there yet but I thought, oh great! I have to sit next to her! How nerve-wracking! How did I get myself into these kinds of situations?

She was late, and the suspense of knowing and not being able to tell anyone tortured me. I asked the mentors, "Is this part of the test?"

They laughed, and one of the mentors said, "You figured that one out."

Lynn finally walked in with her colorful clothes, her glittering purse, and her incredible body. She stood momentarily over my head and glanced in my direction. Our eyes met, and I quickly shied away.

"You're so cute," she said, laughing.

She sat down and asked if we were ready for testing. She somehow brought attention to me, I don't remember how, so that everyone around the table turned to me, eyeing me with a smile. One of the apprentices, who was my roomie last year, said, "Breathe in for four seconds, hold for four, breathe out for four seconds."

"You guys are not helping," I said, and everyone laughed.

Lynn started going around the table with the questions. She directed the last question to me. "You are an oracle in Delphi, Greece," she said. "A broken country. A wounded child. A man with empty pockets comes to you. What's one tool you would give him?"

I thought and thought. "Love," I said.

"Okay, good. But what's something they can use?"

"The act of power so they can begin to change their lives and their environment around."

"Okay, good. What else?"

"The mother energies."

"Oh, they're too much in a dark place for that."

I laughed. "They wouldn't understand that, would they?"

"You mentioned something about their environment. How

would you change their environment?"

I could not answer that. She had to help me.

"I would gather the people and discuss ways to bring positiveness to the area," she said.

"Yeah, but they don't know anything about that. They got themselves where they are now."

"What about a festival or carnival?"

"Oh!"

Later in the day, Nancy pulled me to the side and said, "Lynn said that she doesn't want you to try to prepare."

"I don't even want to think about it!" I said and grew more and more anxious as the time neared. A part of me wanted to flee the retreat and hide in the mountains or at a café.

Leslie called when I was in the room. "I will be with you in an hour."

"Thank you, Leslie," I said. "I know I will feel your energy."

"No, I will be there physically in an hour."

"What?" I screamed, and my roommate asked what was going on. When I told her, we both screamed and jumped on the bed.

Leslie laughed.

"A big weight has been lifted off my chest," I said. "I had been looking for a distraction to get my mind off of tonight, and this is it."

She told us not tell anyone, that she'd surprise us. My roomie and I had a field day after I hung up. We laughed at the power and beauty of Leslie's actions. We imagined her sitting there on a Saturday, looking around the house, looking at the clock, at the dog, then saying, "Fuck it!" as she picked up her keys, got in the car, and took off in what would total an eight-hour drive. She had been sending loads of texts and tagging her apprentices on Facebook, sharing many beautiful sentiments and sending lots of blessings. We could feel how badly she wanted to be with us.

"No cop better stop her on the way or she'll kick his ass," I said, and we laughed and laughed as we continued to imagine Leslie's long curls flying in the car as she passed traffic.

On our walk to the cafeteria, my roommate said, "Do you know why they picked you?"

"They probably think I'm entertaining enough for the job."

We laughed and laughed. In the middle of eating our dinner, Leslie walked into the cafeteria, and my roomie and I jumped to our feet and ran to hug her. Leslie's other apprentices followed us. She sat beside me for a few minutes and said to all her girls, "Come on, finish your food. I want to give you something before the healing circle begins."

We quickly threw out the remainder of our food, put our trays and dishes away, and followed her to the parking lot. The clear sky and shining stars filled the area and mesmerized us, despite the shouting teenagers that could be heard from the lodging behind us. When we got to her car, she opened her trunk. She took out one necklace after another and placed each one around our neck. We made a circle, held each other's hands, and prayed. She then blessed us by placing an ointment on our forehead.

We returned to my room at 7:30 pm. Nancy was there, waiting for us.

Chapter 20
HEALING CIRCLE

W e walked toward Piper Hall, my legs shaking. Leslie had given me her green shawl to wear. Nancy and my roomie held me by each arm while Leslie walked ahead of us. She led the way. I kept praying to Jesus. In Arabic, I thanked him for this opportunity and asked him to please help me, that whatever the purpose for this ceremony it be of benefit to others.

The beating of drums and the sounds of rattles increased as we neared the room where everyone waited for Lynn and the person who would be in the healing circle. I prayed in fast repetition, fear engulfing me in the dark night that felt like the mist of a dream. I took deep breaths, and then the words that entered my heart last year returned – help me help others. That's why I was doing this, I remembered. I needed to do it so that I could empower myself and thus, empower others.

Lynn appeared, and I felt relieved for the distraction. Someone came and put a microphone on me, and Lynn said that I had to remove my necklace. It was the necklace Leslie had gifted me in the parking lot.

"Can't she just place it sideways?" Leslie asked.

"It'll keep hitting the mic," Lynn said.

I removed it and handed it to Leslie, who winked at me. She had stuck one of her shields in my bra earlier. Leslie asked Lynn if she could use her feather fan instead of Lynn's feather fan, and Lynn looked at Leslie's greenish feather fan for a moment and said, "Yes, I can do that."

Lynn then asked to have a word with me, and I stepped with her into a smaller room. She said, "Is there something that you want to talk about today? Maybe something from your childhood?"

"Yesterday when I went into the Labyrinth, I felt like I stepped into the streets of Baghdad. It caught me by surprise because I did not realize that land still has such a strong effect on me."

"Okay, then we'll talk about that."

We headed toward the door with me following and one of her arms around me.

"Should I be scared?" I asked, terrified.

"No."

That did not make me feel any better.

Fiona momentarily opened the entrance door and, when she saw us, quickly closed it again.

"What are they doing in there?" Lynn asked Leslie and Nancy, exasperated.

"They're raising the energy," someone responded.

Soon the doors opened and we walked into the darkness, Lynn's arms around me. I just about froze. My feet moved only because she led the way. My eyes remained in the middle of our path so that I would not see anyone's face. The rattles moved, sticks banged against large drums, peoples' torsos were visible, but not their faces. We arrived to two chairs set in the middle of the room. The chairs were dressed in white fabric and faced each other. Beside them was a table with a bright lamp.

We sat down, and Lynn asked, "How are you?"

"I'm good," I said, smiling wide and thinking, here we go.

"Before we came into this room, you told me about an incident earlier today when you walked the labyrinth. What happened at the labyrinth?"

"As soon as I stepped onto the sand, I remembered my birth place."

"Where's that?"

"Baghdad," I said, my voice choking up.

"What's the matter?"

"I miss Baghdad, and I can't visit there. I cannot go back."

"You miss it?"

"Yes, and I feel guilty, guilty that I left and others suffered."

"What was it like for you in Baghdad?"

"I had a happy childhood."

"You lived in the city?"

"Yes."

"What do you remember about that city?"

"The busy markets, playing outside, walking to the bakery to buy fresh bread, sleeping on the rooftop in the summer where we could see the stars and the moon."

"So going to the market, sleeping under the stars…What else? The Bedouins there are known to have great horses. Did you ever see or ride horses?"

"No, but I did see the Bedouins."

"And you liked living there?"

"Yes. Except for a few incidences, I had a happy childhood."

"What were these incidences?"

"Once, my niece, who is older than me, wanted me to sleep at her house. I told her and my sister that our school was going to Saddam's parade the next day and it was mandatory to attend. My sister said not to worry about it, that nothing serious would happen if I did not go. So I slept at my niece's house, and when I returned to school, the principal called me and another girl who had not come to the parade to the front of the school. She slapped me so hard, I passed out. This was the first time anyone had hit me."

"So you lived under a harsh regime and were lucky to have left."

"Yes," I said, the word *lucky* standing out for me.

"That world that is in your mind is not what it's like now," she said, her voice and demeanor resembling that of my mother when she'd warned me not to visit Iraq, that the Iraq in my head is not the one in real life.

"What did your father do in Iraq?"

"He was the head of the accounting department at the railway station and he was a bonesetter."

"A what?"

"A bonesetter."

"What's that?"

"When people broke their legs or other parts of their body, they went to him to fix it. He did it for free."

"So he was a healer?"

"Yes."

"Was he Muslim?"

"No, we're Christian."

She straightened herself in the chair. "Okay, so what happened after that school incident?"

"Not long after, we came to America."

"How was that for you?"

I felt pressure in my throat, and I said, bursting into tears, "Things got worse."

"How did they get worse?"

"I didn't even know until we got here that we were not going back to Iraq, that I would never see my friends, my school, or my neighborhood again," I said, crying. "I never got to say goodbye to my friends. We left in secrecy."

"Is this why you avoid getting close to people?"

I was quiet, taken aback by her question and seeing for the first time how I did protect myself by always keeping some distance.

"Did your parents ever talk to you about the move and what was going on?" she asked.

"No."

"Why not?"

"I don't know."

"I want you to close your eyes and tell me how it felt when you came here."

I closed my eyes and instantly saw the house in Shelby Township. "It was dark. We lived in the suburbs, and there were never people outside. Everyone stayed inside. There was food everywhere. It was strange, to have access to food all day long. I felt lonely and isolated, and I turned to food for comfort. I got fat."

"How was it in school? How did people treat you?"

"The teachers were good and the students...some were good, some bad."

I had opened my eyes by this point, and she told me to close them. She asked, "What else happened?"

"My father died," I said, again bursting into tears and hearing the gush of the microphone as I placed my hand on my heart in memory of him. The drumming and rattling intensified, and the room became hotter. I noticed this happened whenever I went deeper, said something painful. Their performance resembled that of a professional mourner in Mediterranean and Near Eastern cultures. Since biblical times, a woman skilled at storytelling evoked mourners at funerals to lament their grief to the fullest. Traditionally, the woman chosen for this sacred task knew the family and the deceased person well so she could easily give a heartfelt, tear-jerking eulogy. In modern days, people hired professional mourners.

Some time passed before Lynn asked sympathetically, "What happened?"

"He got sick and weak after he came here. He was not happy here. He came to this country so his children would have a better future."

"Did you feel guilty about his death?"

I thought about that for a moment. "I don't know. I just know that he went from being healthy and active to his body quickly deteriorating."

"What about your mother?"

"She was happy here, because her children were in a safer place."

"Did she work?"

"No, she never worked outside the home."

I felt Lynn clearing energy from my chest with the feather fan Leslie had handed her. "Okay, I want you to see beautiful light from the sun…"

My face softened as the rays of sunlight thoroughly immersed the large kitchen's bay windows in Shelby's house, where I would often stand and look outside at the green grass or white snow. My parents and siblings often gathered in that kitchen. Our family began to fall apart right around that time.

"You are married, right?"

"Yes."

"You're happy with your husband?"

"Yes."

"Are you sure?"

"Yes."

"How did you two meet?"

"I visited Iraq in 2000, and he proposed. I said no. He came to America four years later and proposed again. I said yes."

"He loves you?"

"Yes," I said, smiling. "He is from my tribe."

"He is from your tribe?"

"Yes, he's from our relations."

"Who is your tribe?"

"They're the Chaldeans, the Christians of Iraq," I said.

"How big is your tribe?"

I thought about it, counting my family and his. First I thought fifty but realized we were much more than that. I said, "Eighty."

"Where are they from?"

"My parents and grandparents and his parents and grandparents were born in a village in northern Iraq. It was taken by ISIS last year."

"Oh, honey. You are so lucky, so lucky to have left."

Each time she said the word "lucky," I thought about my attachment to Baghdad, whose beauty no longer existed except in my head. The Hanging Gardens, Ishtar Gate, Ziggurat of Ur, Babylon City, and all the biblical stories were an old story. I wondered how much of this attachment interfered with my happiness.

"When you went back in 2000, did you go inside the house where you lived and did you visit your friends?"

"I went to the house, but I was not able to go inside."

"Why not?"

"They wouldn't let us…"

"They wouldn't?" she asked, surprised.

"They did not trust us."

"How about your friends? Did you see them?"

"No."

"Why not?"

"They had left the country too. One came to the United States, and I don't know where the other one is."

"So they were lucky to get out too."

I smiled. "Yes."

"You have children?"

"A nine-year-old daughter and a six-year-old son."

"That's interesting that your daughter is the same age that you were when you left Iraq."

We were quiet momentarily.

"Are you happy?" she asked.

"I'm happy with my family, but I have too many responsibilities."

"You have too many responsibilities?"

"My mother lives with us. She's in a wheelchair."

"Why is she in a wheelchair?"

"She doesn't walk."

"Why doesn't she walk?"

"She gave up on life."

"She was happier here because her children were safer, so why did she give up on life?"

I remembered her attachment to her sons and the custom that made her believe she would live old age in one of their homes. "She fell ill after she moved out of my brother's home," I said.

"I want you to close your eyes and tell me, where is Baghdad in your body?"

"My heart."

"Where is the pain of that responsibility in your body?"

"In my stomach."

"What do you see there, to your right side?"

There was a heavy darkness and a pressure inside of me that caused me to keep squirming in my chair. I wanted to break like an egg, the yolk and whites dropping to the floor, no longer contained in one place. A funnel cloud then appeared, picking up speed and whirling around until it grew bigger and higher.

"I see a tornado."

"What's the tornado doing?" she asked.

"I'm the tornado. I've become the tornado to contain everything that's happening around me."

"How did you become the tornado?"

"Through submission and acceptance."

"Does this tornado do any damage?"

"No."

"Are you angry at your mother?"

The question aroused an inner fire. The flames must have been like a wallpaper on my face, because she said, "Oh honey, you're in so much pain."

"I'm angry at the situation," I said. "I was honored to have my mother live with me, but now I'm tired."

"You're tired?"

"Yes."

"You said your mom had twelve children. Where are the rest of them?"

"They live blocks or a few miles away."

"Blocks away! Do they help?"

I stayed quiet.

"Why don't you ask them to help? She's their mother too."

"I don't know."

She asked someone to bring her a drum. The drum arrived, and she said, "I want you to drum your anger into this drum."

Someone placed the drum in my lap. I had never really drummed using a Native American drum. I started with small, gentle beats that grew stronger and louder and stronger and louder, leading the orchestration of the rest of the room's drumming and rattling. It drew my mind away from my emotions as I beat out my anger, not knowing even what I was angry at, before I stopped. The flames extinguished, my head bobbed forward in sorrow and exhaustion.

"When you return home, I want you to ask your family for help," she said.

"Okay."

"I want you to ask your husband to help you," she said.

I looked into her deep blue eyes and felt as if she could see what was in my living room.

"Promise me you will ask him to help you," she emphasized.

"I promise."

The healing circle ceremony over, one of the women came to undo the mic. I got up, and Lynn placed the shawl over my head, covering my eyes slightly. As we walked around, different people hugged me. Some were even crying. One woman, a first-year apprentice, said, "I'm so lucky I met you." One of the apprentices from Germany, a classmate, kissed me on both cheeks and my lips, and I felt tears on her face. "You are such a courageous woman! I had no idea what you had gone through." Other classmates had similar words and reactions. Fiona hugged me tight and when I saw Janet, I fell into her embrace, weeping, because she reminds me of a grandmother, the grandmother I did not have.

On the way out, the woman who had handed me the drum was standing at the door. She said, "You can keep the drum."

I was led outside, Nancy on one side and my roommate on the other. During our walk toward our room, the woman who gifted me the drum called for us to wait. We turned and saw one of the mentors open the door. Leslie came out of it shortly afterward and followed us. I found myself crying harder as I tucked my head into Nancy's embrace.

Back in the room, I lay in bed, Nancy beside me as I sobbed. I felt like a child being held by her mother. I needed Nancy's caring and nurturing so badly, so so badly. I had taken on so much weight over the years and felt that there was no one to relieve my burden. My cries increased, and I could feel my roommate and Leslie massaging my body to comfort me. Leslie said to let it all out, buggers, snots and all, and I continued to cry until she said, "Come on, Weam, I know you can do better than that."

That was when I burst into laughter. I sat up, and we chatted and laughed until the middle of the night. Occasionally I cried whatever tears were left inside of me. At one point, the phone rang. It was my husband, wanting to check if I was all right and to tell me he missed and loved me. I wondered if Lynn had zapped him somehow, since she'd been so adamant about him helping me.

Nancy, Leslie, and my roomie told me I was taking on way too much and that I needed to ask for help. They mentioned different ways to ask for help, but nothing clicked. I kept feeling that once I was home, I wouldn't be able to ask for it.

I didn't remember what time Nancy left the room, but once she was gone, Leslie told me to take a shower. When I came out with a towel around my body, she said, "You didn't wash your hair?"

"No."

"It's protocol that you do that after the healing circle ceremony, to take a bath with essential oils. Since there is no bathtub in the room, I'll just put essential oils on your head."

Leslie stayed in our room that night, and after we went to bed, I woke up when it was still dark, my head pounding with the scene of me sitting on that chair. A few words kept popping up. One in particular drove me crazy. When Lynn asked me, "How big is your tribe?" I answered "Eighty." That was not correct. My tribe was much larger than that. My engagement party alone, which consisted of only immediate family members and first cousins, had 150 guests. My wedding, which included second cousins, was 300 guests, and that was considered a small wedding in comparison to the rest of the Chaldean weddings, which average about 500 guests.

I thought, who gives a shit that I gave the wrong answer? I just want to go back to sleep. Please God let me sleep. I'm tired, and my head is going to explode. But the "wrong" answer kept whirling in my head, and I could not stand the thought that I had given the "wrong" answer to Lynn, and in front of all those people too. I tried to get up and find something to do to distract my thoughts, but my body was too tired. My legs were sore from the shaking they went through during the time leading to the healing circle.

Then it came to me. I remembered the time that I was called in class to answer a science question. The teacher said that if we did not know the answer to this question, she would send us to the principal's office. This terrified me. I had, by now, tasted the wrath of this principal and the last thing I wanted was to go through that again. I prayed the teacher would not call on me.

The teacher called my name, and I stood. She asked the question, and I could not answer. I froze, and she told me to go to the principal's office. The principal, her mean face looking at me with rage, asked, "Why didn't you know the answer?" Before I could answer, she slapped me with all her might. This time I did not pass out, but I burst into tears. It was the second time someone had ever hit me.

It now dawned on me that I was hit twice during the same school year because, in both instances, my classroom and the teacher were the same. These incidences occurred when Saddam came into power in the late 1970s, and the energy in the school shifted. I remembered that even after the first time the principal hit me, and I woke up in my classroom, the teacher who tried to be nice to me had a strange smile, like a grin. When she called me to answer the question and I could not, that same grin appeared because she knew what would follow. When I remembered those days, I had assumed she was a nice teacher who felt bad for me, but I always felt discomfort about that smile of hers. I wondered now if she had purposely called upon me to answer the question, seeing from the expression on my worried face that I did not know the answer and as a result would receive a blow.

Then I realized how the accidents I had of wetting my bed occurred during this same time. All these years I had attributed these accidents to me being a late bloomer when in reality, they were the result of the principal's abuse. One day I had also skipped school, simply sat against someone's front yard fence until it was time to return home. In my adulthood, I thought this was due to being an introvert who yearned to spend time alone. I was made to believe that if I got anything wrong, there was punishment, consequences, that I would get hit.

Growing up under Saddam's regime, fear crawled onto our skin, homes, and streets like the tiny bird mites that once attacked me in the thousands. The fear itself was so small you could not see it, not even under a microscope, but in accumulation, in millions, it swelled your character with discomfort and paranoia that was challenging to get rid of. These types of tyrannical mites, even after you exterminated them, their bite marks on their prey remain.

Chapter 21
THE MORNING AFTER
THE HEALING CIRCLE

In the morning, Leslie grabbed her purse and said she had to buy coffee from Starbucks. I said I'd come with her. We were both in our pajamas. In the car, before leaving the parking lot, she stopped to take a picture of the sun rising between two trees. We drove and ran into one of the apprentices, who was sitting outside smoking a cigarette.

"You have to stop smoking," Leslie said to her.

The apprentice laughed. "I'm quitting when I go home."

As we drove into the street, Leslie checked her phone and said to herself, "I know there's a Starbucks around here." A star lit on her iPhone map. She drove, commenting how there were many Catholic sanctuaries here and what a lovely area it was. The affluent neighborhood was lovely and the street's landscape, especially the palm trees, resembled the beautiful suburbs in Iraq. No wonder I immediately connected to Iraq when I set foot onto the sand in the labyrinth. This place had elements familiar to Baghdad: the dry sand, the fruit and palm trees, the warm weather.

"Shit, they don't have drive-through," Leslie said.

"I'll go in," I said. Even though we were both in our pajamas, hers were a silk black nightgown just above her knees with a robe, and mine were pants and a shirt.

She wanted to pay from her prepaid card, but I refused, said it was my treat.

We drove back to the retreat. I grabbed my notebook and pen and sat outside on a bench to write in my journal. The gay man was walking when I stopped him and asked him to take a picture of me, jokingly warning him that it better turn out right. A woman in her early forties showed up. She had red hair with a number of braids and wore a straw hat. She said, "I honor you for the courage to speak yesterday. It was healing for us too."

"I was nervous about seeing everyone today because I felt so exposed yesterday, like I'd be walking naked into the cafeteria," I said.

The man laughed. "Like we'd be pointing our finger at you and be like, oh she's the one, did you see what she said last night?"

"Yes!"

"I think Lynn wanted us to see a global perspective on what's happening in the world, how war and immigration impact people," the man said.

My mother often said to me, "May everything that you touch turn to gold."

For centuries, immigrants coming to America expected to see streets paved in gold. When they arrived, this romantic idea quickly turned into a raging sizzle. In search of the gold, many became pessimistic and labeled the American dream a myth. But the American dream is not a bed sheet covering the streets like a bed. It's within us. Living in the land of opportunity gives dreams possibilities for growth and realization. Dreaming, like everything else, is work. There's a process to it, and like shamanism or any other course of study, it cannot be bought or learned impatiently. It requires patience, persistence, tenacity, and belief. It has to be earned.

My parents had brought their children here to experience freedom. Anything more than that was topping on the cake.

We talked and laughed for a little bit, and I realized I need not feel embarrassed about the amount of emotions I'd released the night before. I truly was surrounded by a loving group of people who did not intend to criticize me or make me feel bad in any way. They wanted to embrace me and help heal my wounds.

I returned to the room to get ready. I looked at my natural curls in the mirror.

"I avoided washing my hair yesterday because my sister had straightened it to last for the trip," I said to Leslie. "But then you forced me to."

"Why don't you leave it like that, since your natural beauty is God given?" she asked.

I thought about that and realized that, for too many years, I had tried to fit into the Chaldean cultures' ways, which were filled with insecurities and materialism. I dressed up and looked good, but I felt a pressure I could not understand and wanted desperately to free myself from. I looked at my curls differently, with admiration, and then left the room and strode to the cafeteria. When I got there, the apprentices from my school year embraced me and said I looked really good.

I smiled. "It's because I washed my hair."

"No, it's not because you washed your hair," they said. The woman from Spain added, "Last night, I couldn't believe how quickly your face expression could transform. One minute you look stoic, with an ancient soul. Another moment you're very innocent, like a child."

Lisa, the other apprentice who went through Chip and

Susan's teachings with me, had once described me exactly like that.

After breakfast, we prepared for the graduation ceremony, where each apprentice got to walk underneath the elk skin that was gifted to Lynn by her teacher. As I neared that elk skin, each year of the school whispered through my body. I re-experienced the tears, love, and warmth of the work, and when I stepped out of the elk skin, Lynn handed me a certificate of completion. I hugged and thanked her as she congratulated me.

When I graduated high school, I did not walk at commencements. I did not view my high school diploma as much of an accomplishment. When, three years later, I received my bachelor's degree from Wayne State University, I again did not walk at commencements. Although I enjoyed my college years and was happy to attain my degree, I felt there was something missing. I had a deep desire to learn more about real life and myself that seemed beyond what formal education could teach.

For the next two decades, I studied with various spiritual masters and took umpteen writing courses. All were wonderful experiences that helped me grow and flourish as a person and a writer, but most importantly, they led me to an extraordinary school, Lynn Andrews' four-year shamanic school. I had initially signed up to the school to find my literary voice, which had gotten lost due to the pains of witnessing the Iraq war and dealing with my enormous responsibilities as a wife and new mother.

I had no idea then that the school's ancient teachings would not only heal old wounds that had muffled my literary voice, but that it would also improve my relationship with the Great Spirit, with myself, and with my family. The work was mystical but also very intense and challenging. I had to put my heart and soul into my family, home, and career while doing the schoolwork because the purpose of these teachings is to incorporate what we learn into every aspect of our daily life.

I graduated, but as they say, "The end is always followed by a new beginning."

Chapter 22
A DAZZLING TALE

Before I went to Storm Eagle, my sister had a dream about me. She said that she rarely remembered her dreams, but this one was so vivid, she could not forget it. In the dream, I was belly dancing in a way she'd never seen me dance before, with my head lifted in happiness and confidence. My posture was straight and strong, my breasts set high, and my moves were so complicated that she worried I'd fall but it was obvious to her I would not fall. She wondered, "Could yoga have done this for her body?" She was amazed as she watched me belly dance in ecstasy in a "professional" manner she did not know was in me.

That was what occurred after Storm Eagle. Healing time now over, I began to stand tall, with shoulders back and down, chest up, as I took long strides. Healing time is never meant to be a permanent stance, but a place to get better so we can get back in the game. It's important to get in touch with our dark side and then expose it to the light. That's how we become victors rather than victims over our lives and create dazzling tales for ourselves and the generations that will follow.

In the middle of the year, I had created a space in my home to work one-on-one with people. My husband was encouraging, had even said, "You're good at that." I realized that neither he, nor Leslie's husband, were clueless at all. They had seen us blossom into our true selves and applauded us for it. Leslie had simply said and done what she did to pacify my then tense relationship with my husband.

Before the end of the year, I made sure to plan for a big celebration that incorporated all my five years' hard work. I booked a family trip to Cancun, Mexico. We arrived to the country in late January. We swam with the dolphins, visited the locals, danced to Latin music, and enjoyed quality time together.

"Mayan people did not leave the Earth with aliens to another planet," said our tour guide as our bus drove us to the Coba Ruins in Tulum. "They are still here, making handmade items. Each family-owned store supports almost fifty people."

When we arrived to the ruins, the tour guide explained that Maya was not an empire. It was a city of 70,000 people with smaller cities within the bigger city, but not a place where one person ruled over everyone. Their classical era was between 400 to 900 AD. During that time, men who had knowledge controlled people by keeping them ignorant and using this knowledge to make the ignorant people believe in them.

So, those who knew about solstice and equinox, which occurs twice a year, would make predictions based on this information and would credit this prediction to his close relationship to God, who he communicated with by going to the top of the temple. They claimed that the God of Rain, or whatever god, delivered information to this or that special person.

I remembered a conversation I once had with the Red Indian about community. I'd said to him, "You once said that things are changing, that people are becoming more aware."

"More people are waking up. We can talk about current events. Since 1992, history has been changing. People are more concerned with smaller communities instead of federations.

Instead of being one world order, one guy telling the world what to do – how stupid – most people are going toward communities with families, not some fat cat telling you where you're going to work and when you're going to come home. They are becoming more conscientious of their neighborhood. The time for making a mess is over. People are not happy with that, not for themselves, not for their grandparents, not for their children or their cousins.

"The wisest thing on this earth is common sense. People go into the moon when it's all there in front of you. They think if you pay a lot then it's the best for you. If you do something and the community enjoys it, then it's a good thing. Whatever you do, the community has to enjoy it. Otherwise, it doesn't mean anything."

"So, is there really sovereignty anywhere?" I asked.

"People don't govern themselves. People serve God. That's the problem with this country. The word sovereignty is a nasty word. It means to reign over. You're sovereign to your children right now but when they come of age, then you should not sovereign over them. Let them go and discover the Creator. They made the word sovereign sound good. They want you to say, I am sovereign over myself. As soon as you say that, you give up the Creator. I am not sovereign. I need help and other things.

"In English, God is dog spelled backwards. Those who made the English language created that word, God. There is no God for them. They are God. Period. And they are serious. Every time you say God, you are referring to dog, which is manmade because there were no dogs in North America. They brought it with them. That's their God. God might not be him. It might be her. Or it might be not her or him. God is God."

"I remember you telling me once about the word God being

'dog' spelled backwards. I will research the roots of both words and your theory of how they're associated."

"You are looking for answers in their words, and you'll find their answers to these questions. 'Don't believe me. You watch and see.' That's what my father told me, and he was always right."

My mother often brought up God's name. Once I asked her, "Who helped you raise your twelve children?" She thought for a moment and then responded, "God."

"And you can write all this and say it's yours," the Red Indian continued.

"No, I won't do that."

"No, do it. You can."

"No, I write memoirs, true stories, which I think is more fascinating than making things up. I don't even know why people make things up. It's less interesting to do that."

"The spirit of the air, that's why people make things up. There are people who were cast here, and people who were lowered. Native people were lowered here by creation. *Ishnaibai* were lowered here to write and watch and help those who were cast here so that they don't hurt themselves. Some people just make things up and are giddy about stupid shit that doesn't mean anything to anyone. Some are ninety years old and they can easily act as though they are a seven-year-old child, and those are the ones you have to look out for, especially when the ninety year olds who are actually seven have lots of money, because they think they can buy anything, and they can. Then there are people who write serious and important things, and no one believes it."

He paused, then quickly added, in a cheerier tone, "But anyway, you can write this and say it's yours."

"No, I don't want to do that. I don't know any of this stuff.

I just like to share what I receive, and if it does any good, I did my job."

"You can write it and say you dreamt it or something."

"Well, I've had dreams, but not about these things. My dreams just tell me what to do, who to talk to, and I follow."

He then said he had something for me. "I can show it to you, you can write about what's in it, but you can't have it because there isn't another one like it."

"I can't buy it?" I asked.

"I'm not a shaman. I'm not for sale." He chuckled. "You can't find it in the stars. It's for you."

"Okay."

"I've met you before."

"I know. You told me that before."

"I met you before."

"I know."

The tour guide talked about the Mayan sacred book, which mentions the World Tree. That's a magical tree that creates the four sacred directions that go around the center. It's a structure for humans that shapes and accesses the spiritual worlds. According to their belief, the World Tree was the first creation and then everything emanated, and continues to emanate, from it.

"Now we are going to go see the Coba archeological site and, if you want, you can go up the 120 steps."

He then explained that we had three options to get to the ruins: one, walk there; two, rent a bicycle; three, rent a Mayan limo, a chauffeured tricycle where you just sit and take in the sights. We opted for the limo, which my children, even myself, found more adventurous than climbing the Coba ruins' 120 steps, which we also did, huffing and puffing.

We later went into a cenote, one of many underwater caves in the Yucatan, using a Mayan elevator. Mayan men tied each tourist individually with ropes and brought us down to salt water which was so fresh, the locals drank from it, so we had to remove all and any suntan lotion or other chemicals we had on our bodies. We also went zip lining in the Yucatan Peninsula, which consists largely of the ancient Maya Lowlands with many Maya archaeological sites such as the Chichen Itza, Tulum, and Uxmal. In modern history, it was largely a cattle ranching, logging, chicle and henequen production area. Since the 1970s, and the fall of the world henequen and chicle market due to the advent of synthetic subtitles, the Yucatan Peninsula's economy has relied more on tourism.

Due to this, we were able to enjoy a stroll in a Mayan town, have lunch at a family-owned Mayan restaurant, and experience several ceremonies with Mayan shamans, which for me was the most delightful adventure. Observing the Mayans, I thought of my ancestors' children, the ones God had gathered in the city of my current habitation. Lynn had repeatedly said that I was lucky, and she was right.

Chapter 23
BLESSED BY MAYAN SHAMANS

It was a full moon, a Wolf Moon. Before 3 pm, I walked to the trail leading to the Mayan ceremony. I came upon a narrow pathway to the right, where there was a bowl of incense beside a large shell sitting on the ground to welcome attendees. Over it, a sign read:

"Enjoy a relaxing experience and feel yourself being reborn with this mystical old-age rite. The Temazcal steam bath is good for the soul. It mixes a spiritual journey with a truly delightful encounter with the basic elements of our planet: water, fire, earth, and wind…"

I walked down the narrow road that seemed hidden within the beautiful trees. The road led to a round area where three men dressed in white trousers prepared the burning of large black stones. They greeted me and asked that I take a seat on the bench, beside an Indian couple who also happened to live in Michigan. I then watched as the men continued to make the black stones hotter and redder.

During the ceremony, we had the opportunity to reflect on our negativities and then to throw them away, using maple syrup chips, into the incense bowl that the shaman came to us with. We drank a bowl of tree sap, were asked to close our eyes and dream in our new vision, and we were blessed by the shaman in the Mayan language. Then we were led into a sweat lodge.

The sweat lodge was dark, with only four lit candles. Soon the hot stones were brought in by a wagon and piled in the middle of the room. The room became warm, and when the men poured aromatic water over the stones, producing steam, it became hotter and hotter.

"I will eventually blow out the candles, and the room will be completely dark," he said, both in English and Spanish so all seven people would understand him. "If you feel you want to leave, that's okay. Just clap your hands and we will help you out. But I ask that you stay and take advantage of this opportunity. Allow the prayers to transport you to another place in time. Allow the steam created by the herbs and hot stones to envelope your body as it purifies your spirit, then experience a rebirth as you abandon to the warm shelter of mother earth's womb."

He talked about the feminine power, the importance of women in this world, how they are the backbone of society and therefore needs to be treated well by men. He then talked about the four elements of our planet. Not long after he blew out the candles, with the steam rising higher and the room getting hotter, I did have an urge to escape, to clap my hands. I tried to stay still, but I felt very uncomfortable, and then I asked myself, "What am I afraid of?"

Suddenly, I relaxed. I relaxed enough to listen to all my teachers' wisdom. To have abundance, you have to feel abundance. You have to be grateful. When you relax and feel you have enough, you have enough. People who are powerful dreamers cannot drop an ounce of their energy. They must sift through and contain their energy and accept all parts of themselves. We have to change our realities before we can change anyone else's realities. You can't just dream. You have to manifest the dream.

This helped me see that everything I've been doing my whole life led to this moment and that every single moment is important. I had found my voice, owned my stories, and as Lynn had taught me to do, became proud of my perceptions and my willingness to write and grow. I was lucky to have studied with Lynn, and I didn't want to stop that flow of energy. I had to share it because we are one big family who came from one man and one woman. What one knows, the other knows. All we have to do is use the tools, such as memory, imagination, and rational thinking, to gather ourselves into a collaborative consciousness.

We walked out of the sweat lodge into a waterfall of pure water. We returned to the circle for another drink and to give gratitude. The shaman thanked us for keeping this thousand-year-old Mayan tradition alive with our participation. We thanked him for this amazing opportunity.

The last time I had gone to Mexico was twenty years ago, to chaperone my niece and her friends for their Spring Break. Back then, shamans were not a part of any excursion. Back then, few people had ever heard the word *shaman.* Luckily, a lot has changed. Today the tradition of shamanism is not only alive and well, but it's available to everyone who understands and appreciates the healing and rejuvenation it provides for us and our Earth.

My story had come full circle and found its end, but the teachings never ended. They had only now begun.

The End

OTHER BOOKS BY WEAM NAMOU

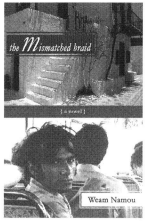

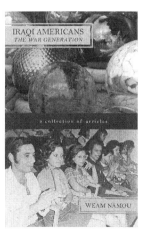

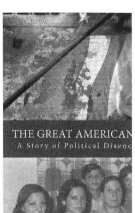

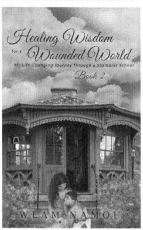

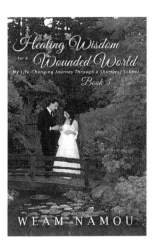

The Feminine Art
(ISBN-13: 978-0975295625)
A novel about a married woman who distracts herself from boredom by trying to find her nephew a wife

The Mismatched Braid
(ISBN-13: 978-0975295632)
A novel about an Iraqi refugee living in Athens who falls in love with his American cousin

The Flavor of Cultures
(ISBN-13: 978-0975295663)
A novel about a Chaldean girl in America who tries to find her individuality while maintaining her tribal lifestyle

I Am a Mute Iraqi with a Voice
(ISBN-13: 978-0975295694)
A collection of 76 poems

The Great American Family: A Story of Political Disenchantment
(ISBN-13: 978-0977679058)
Through a single case, Namou touches on a number of important issues that are robbing American families from living the American dream

Iraqi Americans: The War Generation
(ISBN-13: 978-0977679096)
A collection of 36 articles that Namou wrote over the years which paint a picture of Iraqi Americans' political and social situation and their struggles

Iraqi Americans: Witnessing a Genocide
(ISBN-13: 978-0977679072)
A nonfiction book that provides the Iraqi American view on Iraq and the Islamic State

Iraqi Americans: The Lives of the Artists
(ISBN-13: 978-0977679010)
A book about the rich lives of 16 artists who are of Mesopotamian descent

Healing Wisdom for a Wounded World
My Life-Changing Journey Through a Shamanic School
(Book 1)
(ISBN 978-0977679041)
Namou's memoir about her first-year apprenticeship in a 4-year shamanic school that is founded and run by bestselling author and mystic Lynn Andrews.

Healing Wisdom for a Wounded World
My Life-Changing Journey Through a Shamanic School
(Book 2)
ISBN-13: 978-1945371998
Namou's memoir about her second-year apprenticeship in a
4-year shamanic school that is founded and run by bestselling
author and mystic Lynn Andrews.

Healing Wisdom for a Wounded World
My Life-Changing Journey Through a Shamanic School
(Book 3)
ISBN 978-1-945371-97-4
Namou's memoir about her third-year apprenticeship in a
4-year shamanic school that is founded and run by bestselling
author and mystic Lynn Andrews.

ATTRIBUTIONS

About the Author

Living in the twenty-first century, many people feel stressed and overwhelmed by life's complexities. They want to find their purpose in life. For over 25 years, I have traveled extensively and worked with wise and diverse masters who passed on teachings I would love to pass on to you through one-on-one sessions, workshops, and speaking engagements.

If you would like to learn more about how to add meaning to your life by applying this ancient wisdom, please visit my website: www.weamnamou.com or email me at Weam@WeamNamou.com

Made in the USA
Middletown, DE
12 October 2016